# Photoshop® Elements 7
## Top 100

# Simplified®

### TIPS & TRICKS

by Rob Sheppard

Visual

WILEY
Wiley Publishing, I

# Photoshop® Elements 7: Top 100 Simplified® Tips & Tricks

Published by
Wiley Publishing, Inc.
10475 Crosspoint Boulevard
Indianapolis, IN 46256
www.wiley.com

Published simultaneously in Canada

Copyright © 2009 by Wiley Publishing, Inc., Indianapolis, Indiana

Library of Congress Control Number: 2009923967

ISBN: 978-0-470-43636-3

Manufactured in the United States of America

10 9 8 7 6 5 4 3 2 1

## Trademark Acknowledgments

## Contact Us

For general information on our other products and services contact our Customer Care Department within the U.S. at 877-762-2974, outside the U.S. at 317-572-3993, or fax 317-572-4002.

For technical support please visit www.wiley.com/techsupport.

WILEY

Wiley Publishing, Inc.

**U.S. Sales**

Contact Wiley at (877) 762-2974 or fax (317) 572-4002.

# PRAISE FOR VISUAL BOOKS

"I have to praise you and your company on the fine products you turn out. I have twelve Visual books in my house. They were instrumental in helping me pass a difficult computer course. Thank you for creating books that are easy to follow. Keep turning out those quality books."
*Gordon Justin (Brielle, NJ)*

"What fantastic teaching books you have produced! Congratulations to you and your staff. You deserve the Nobel prize in Education. Thanks for helping me understand computers."
*Bruno Tonon (Melbourne, Australia)*

"A Picture Is Worth A Thousand Words! If your learning method is by observing or hands-on training, this is the book for you!"
*Lorri Pegan-Durastante (Wickliffe, OH)*

"Over time, I have bought a number of your 'Read Less - Learn More' books. For me, they are THE way to learn anything easily. I learn easiest using your method of teaching."
*José A. Mazón (Cuba, NY)*

"You've got a fan for life!! Thanks so much!!"
*Kevin P. Quinn (Oakland, CA)*

"I have several books from the Visual series and have always found them to be valuable resources."
*Stephen P. Miller (Ballston Spa, NY)*

"I have several of your Visual books and they are the best I have ever used."
*Stanley Clark (Crawfordville, FL)*

"Like a lot of other people, I understand things best when I see them visually. Your books really make learning easy and life more fun."
*John T. Frey (Cadillac, MI)*

"I have quite a few of your Visual books and have been very pleased with all of them. I love the way the lessons are presented!"
*Mary Jane Newman (Yorba Linda, CA)*

"Thank you, thank you, thank you...for making it so easy for me to break into this high-tech world."
*Gay O'Donnell (Calgary, Alberta,Canada)*

"I write to extend my thanks and appreciation for your books. They are clear, easy to follow, and straight to the point. Keep up the good work! I bought several of your books and they are just right! No regrets! I will always buy your books because they are the best."
*Seward Kollie (Dakar, Senegal)*

"I would like to take this time to thank you and your company for producing great and easy-to-learn products. I bought two of your books from a local bookstore, and it was the best investment I've ever made! Thank you for thinking of us ordinary people."
*Jeff Eastman (West Des Moines, IA)*

"Compliments to the chef!! Your books are extraordinary! Or, simply put, extra-ordinary, meaning way above the rest! THANKYOU THANKYOU THANKYOU! I buy them for friends, family, and colleagues."
*Christine J. Manfrin (Castle Rock, CO)*

# CREDITS

**Sr. Acquisitions Editor**
Jody Lefevere

**Project Editor**
Sarah Hellert

**Technical Editor**
Dennis R. Cohen

**Copy Editor**
Scott Tullis

**Editorial Manager**
Robyn Siesky

**Editorial Assistant**
Laura Sinise

**Business Manager**
Amy Knies

**Sr. Marketing Manager**
Sandy Smith

**Sr. Project Coordinator**
Kristie Rees

**Layout**
Carrie A. Cesavice
Andrea Hornberger

**Graphics**
Ana Carrillo
Ronda David-Burroughs

**Quality Control Technician**
Amanda Graham

**Proofreader**
Christine Sabooni

**Indexer**
Broccoli Information Management

**Vice President and Executive Group Publisher**
Richard Swadley

**Vice President and Executive Publisher**
Barry Pruett

**Composition Director**
Debbie Stailey

# ABOUT THE AUTHOR

**Rob Sheppard** is the author/photographer of more than 25 books, a well-known speaker and workshop leader, and is editor-at-large and columnist for the prestigious *Outdoor Photographer* magazine. As author/photographer, Sheppard has written hundreds of articles about photography and nature, plus books ranging from guides to photography such as *Digital Photography: Top 100 Simplified Tips & Tricks*, 3rd edition, to books about Photoshop including *Adobe Camera Raw for Digital Photographers Only* and *Outdoor Photographer Landscape and Nature Photography with Photoshop CS2*. His Web site is at www.robsheppardphoto.com and his blog is at www.photodigitary.com.

# HOW TO USE THIS BOOK

Photoshop® Elements 7: Top 100 Simplified® Tips & Tricks includes 100 tasks that reveal cool secrets, teach timesaving tricks, and explain great tips guaranteed to make you more productive with Elements. The easy-to-use layout lets you work through all the tasks from beginning to end or jump in at random.

## Who is this book for?

You already know Elements basics. Now you'd like to go beyond, with shortcuts, tricks and tips that let you work smarter and faster. And because you learn more easily when someone *shows* you how, this is the book for you.

## Conventions Used In This Book

### ❶ Steps

This book uses step-by-step instructions to guide you easily through each task. Numbered callouts on every screen shot show you exactly how to perform each task, step by step.

### ❷ Tips

Practical tips provide insights to save you time and trouble, caution you about hazards to avoid, and reveal how to do things in Elements that you never thought possible!

### ❸ Task Numbers

Task numbers from 1 to 100 indicate which lesson you are working on.

### ❹ Difficulty Levels

For quick reference, the symbols below mark the difficulty level of each task.

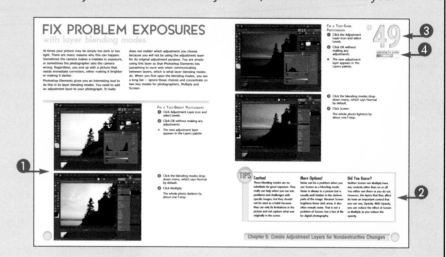

| DIFFICULTY LEVEL | Demonstrates a new spin on a common task |
| DIFFICULTY LEVEL | Introduces a new skill or a new task |
| DIFFICULTY LEVEL | Combines multiple skills requiring in-depth knowledge |
| DIFFICULTY LEVEL | Requires extensive skill and may involve other technologies |

# Table of Contents

# 3 Work with RAW Photos in Photoshop Elements

# 4 Choose Local Control Features

# Table of Contents

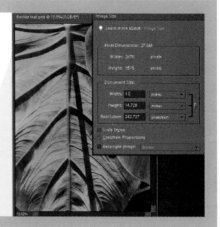

# Table of Contents

# Chapter

# 1

# Organize and Prepare Photos for Processing

Photoshop Elements may be Photoshop's smaller sibling, but it is no second-rate program. Elements uses the same processing engine that Photoshop uses to make your work with photos efficient and effective — it is simpler and directly geared to photographers.

Photoshop Elements is a complete program that allows you to import images, organize them, and sort the good from the bad as well as make changes to optimize individual photos. The order of this book follows a workflow that you can use to work efficiently in Photoshop Elements.

In this chapter, you learn what it means to develop a workflow right from the start. You can quickly import, sort, and organize your pictures so that you can find them more easily in the future. You can customize your workspace to fit your needs and interests and help you work more efficiently. You can also set preferences so that your program works its best. Do not skip over these seemingly mundane tasks because they can really help you speed up your work. However, the best way to work faster in Photoshop Elements is to spend some time with it. Once you have practiced and learned the core controls of the program, you will find that you can work very quickly with Photoshop Elements.

# Top 100

# Develop a
# WORKFLOW

Workflow has become a real buzzword for photographers working with their images in the computer, but it simply describes the process of how you work with images from start to finish. It is important that you develop a consistent way of working on your images that will give you reliable results.

This book is structured in such a way to show you a Photoshop Elements workflow that really does work. Although you can skip around in the book to find specific tips, the book is ordered to follow this workflow. As you become familiar with the program, you might find that you have to adapt some of these ideas to your specific needs. I encourage you to do that as long as you are getting the results you expect from your images. These two pages give a quick overview of a workflow structure.

● Start the process by getting your photos into Photoshop Elements in order to sort, keep, delete, and organize them. You can process individual photos without going into the Organizer module of the program, but the Organizer helps you manage your digital photos.

● Set the tonalities of your photos first, including blacks, whites, and midtones, and then adjust color.

- Fix problems in your photos such as wrong colors, defects in an image, sensor dust, and so on.

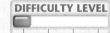

- Consider how you want to share your photos with others, from prints to photo books to Web galleries to e-mail and much more.

---

## TIPS

### Did You Know?

Photoshop Elements was originally designed to make Photoshop more accessible for photographers. Photoshop was originally developed to help people work on photos in the computer, not for photographers. Photoshop Elements has always had the photographer as the primary focus of its development and enhancement.

### Try This!

Make your image immediately fill the central work area by pressing Ctrl+0 (if you press Ctrl+O, you get a file open dialog box). You can do this when a photo first comes into the program edit space or when you have enlarged a portion of the photo and need to go back to seeing all of it.

### Did You Know?

Editing photos used to mean picking the good from the bad. When Photoshop was developed, the computer folks decided to call the changes to the images *editing*, so there is confusion about what editing really is for the photographer. This book avoids both usages and specifically describes the process being used.

---

# IMPORT
## your images

In order to work on your images, you must get them into your computer and recognized by Photoshop Elements. To use the Organizer in Elements, you have to tell the program how to deal with your photos. It needs, in a sense, a map to where your photos are located. Photoshop Elements can help you import your photos from memory card to hard drive, including copying them from the card into a specific folder and renaming the files as well as recognizing

them by Organizer. Or you can tell Elements to recognize photographs that are already on your computer.

When you first open Photoshop Elements, choose the Organizer button to go into that mode. All importing is done through the Organizer mode. Once the Organizer recognizes the images, they show up as thumbnails on your screen and can then be sorted, collected into albums, and more in order to make your pictures very accessible to you.

IMPORTING FROM A DIGITAL CAMERA OR MEMORY CARD

① Click File.

② Click Get Photos and Videos.

③ Click From Camera or Card Reader.

The Photo Downloader dialog box appears.

④ Click the Get Photos From drop-down menu to select your camera or card reader.

⑤ Click Browse to select where you want the photos to go on your hard drive.

Navigate to the folder you want to use in the directory tree that appears.

⑥ Click Make New Folder for a new group of photos.

⑦ Name your new folder.

**DIFFICULTY LEVEL**

⑧ Click to select or create subfolders in the new folder, such as based on dates photos were shot, or choose no subfolders.

⑨ Click to rename your photos or keep the original file name.

⑩ Click to leave photos on the memory card so that your camera can reformat the card properly.

⑪ Click Get Photos.

The photos will now be imported to your computer and included in the Organizer.

**TIPS**

### Did You Know?
A quality memory card reader is the fastest and most dependable way of downloading images. A card reader needs no power, can be left connected to your computer, and will not be damaged if accidentally knocked to the floor.

### Did You Know?
The Automatic Download check box in the Photo Downloader dialog box sets up your computer to automatically download photos based on criteria set in Preferences. This can be a problem because it does not allow you to put photos into specific folders for each download, nor can you rename photos.

### Did You Know?
Most photographers prefer to put images into distinct file folders on their hard drive instead of all lumped together into the Pictures folder. Photo Downloader lets you set up specific folders based on date and location, for example, in a folder called Digital Photos on your hard drive to make them easier to find if the Organizer in Elements ever fails.

# IMPORT
## your images

Sometimes there are groups of photos on your memory card, groups that you do not want to mix together into a single folder. It can be very helpful to keep your photos separated by folders so that you can always find images on your hard drive even without Photoshop Elements. The program gives you the option to import only the pictures that you want from a memory card in an advanced dialog box. This

dialog box is very similar to the Photo Downloader dialog box, but there are some additional choices you should know about.

Photoshop Elements also allows you to import images already on your hard drive. The process is very similar, but does use a different dialog box. This can be useful when you have transferred pictures directly from one computer to another, for example.

### ADVANCED IMPORTING FROM A DIGITAL CAMERA OR MEMORY CARD

①  Repeat steps 1 to 3 from the previous page to open the Photo Downloader dialog box.

②  Click Advanced Dialog.

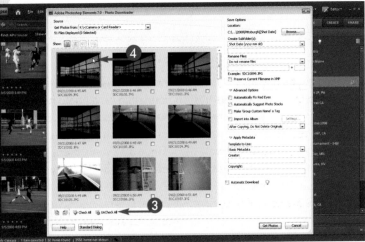

The advanced Photo Downloader dialog box appears.

③  Click Uncheck All to deselect all photos.

④  Click the first photo of your group to import.

**5** Scroll down to the last photo in the group.

**6** Shift+click that last photo to select all from the first one, but no others.

You can Ctrl+click isolated photos to add or remove them from the group.

**CONTINUED**

**7** Click the check box under any image to check all that are selected (☐ changes to ☑).

**8** Click to open Advanced Options if not already open.

● A good option to choose is Import into Album (☐ changes to ☑) if you have albums set up.

**9** Click to open Apply Metadata if not already open.

**10** Click here to select Basic Metadata.

**11** Add your name for Creator and Copyright.

**12** Click Get Photos.

The photos will now be imported to your computer and included in the Organizer.

**TIPS**

### Did You Know?
When the Organizer recognizes photos, Elements does not move or change them unless you tell it to. Photoshop Elements is simply creating a map to these image files on your hard drive so that it can find and organize the photos as needed.

### Try This!
Use the light bulb icons ( 💡 ). Photoshop Elements scatters tips throughout the program to help you when you do not understand a particular control or option. Click the icon and a tip offers you information on how to use the control or option.

### Did You Know?
Having your name and copyright information on a photo helps people keep track of your photos. Even if you are not a pro, having your name in the metadata means that if you give your photo files to someone, such as for an organization's brochure, everyone will know whose photos they are.

# SORT
## the good pictures from the bad

Traditionally, going through your pictures, finding the good ones and getting rid of the bad ones, was called photo editing. However, when computer engineers developed programs like Photoshop, they decided to call changing pictures in those programs photo editing, too, so the term can seem confusing. Still, you do need to go through your pictures and edit them based on the original definition of the word.

Photoshop Elements gives you some excellent tools to do just that. You can compare pictures, look at pictures in different sizes, and discover which pictures work well for you and which do not. To save hard drive space and eliminate clutter there, you should delete images that really do not satisfy you, thus reducing the number of pictures you have to go through to find the really good ones.

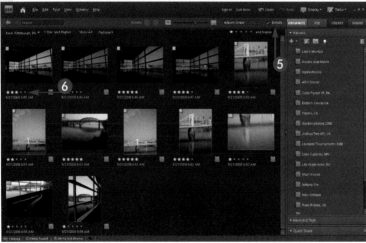

SET UP YOUR VIEW OF THE PHOTOS

1 Click and drag the thumbnail slider to change the sizes of your photo thumbnails.

2 Click Full Screen View to see a photo displayed over the whole screen.

3 Ctrl+click photos to select images that you want to rotate.

4 Click the appropriate Rotate icon to rotate the selected photos.

5 Click the Details check box to show ratings (■ changes to ☑).

*Note: You can also click the View menu and then View Details to show ratings.*

6 Click the dots to rate your photos.

You can use a system such as 1 star for reject, 5 stars for best photos, and other stars to define which you like or dislike.

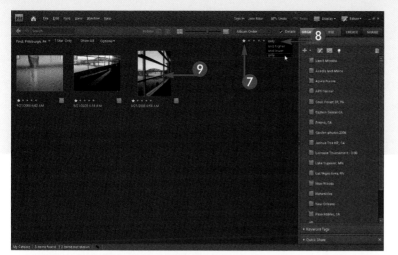

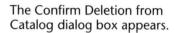

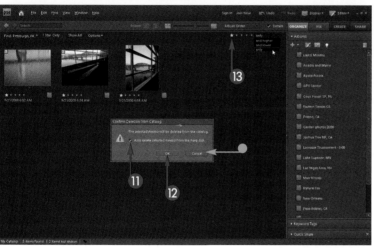

⑦ Click rating star 1 at the upper right of the thumbnail display.

⑧ To limit photos to only those with one star, click the drop-down menu to the right of the stars and select only.

⑨ Select all photos with Ctrl+A.

⑩ Press Delete.

The Confirm Deletion from Catalog dialog box appears.

⑪ Check the box for Also delete selected item(s) from the hard disk to throw out your rejects (■ changes to ✓).

Make sure that the box for Also delete selected item(s) from the hard disk is unchecked to only remove photos from Photoshop Elements view (✓ changes to ■).

● If you feel that you made a mistake, you can click Cancel and change the ratings.

⑫ Click OK to finish the process.

⑬ Click the upper right stars to get your photos in view again.

# 3

DIFFICULTY LEVEL

---

## TIPS

### Remember!

You can delete images from Photoshop Elements and/or off your computer altogether. Simply select the image you want to remove and press the Delete key. This opens a dialog box that lets you decide if you simply want to remove the photo from Photoshop Elements' view or remove it off of the hard drive completely.

### Try This!

To see any image at a large size, double-click it. This shows you the photo filling the thumbnail area without any other photos. This helps you better see details in your photos, such as sharpness or exposure problems. Double-click again to go back to the thumbnail view.

### Did You Know?

You can show file names and other detail by using the View menu. Click View and then select the appropriate menu item to show you what you need to see in your thumbnail display.

---

# CREATE ALBUMS
## to group your pictures

*Albums* are groupings of pictures based on your needs. You can create albums based on events such as birthdays, locations such as a recently visited city, family members, and much more.

Albums give you a way of quickly finding pictures throughout even a very large collection of images. They also allow you to group pictures together even if they were not taken at the same time. For example, you could set up an album based on a child's name

and then put images that have that child in them into that album. If you kept doing this over time, you would have a collection of images of that child from many different times and places.

Albums do not duplicate photographs. They only create references to where the pictures are on your hard drive. For that reason, individual pictures could be in many albums, which can help you find them faster in different ways.

① Ctrl+click photos to select individual images, or click a photo and then Shift+click the last image in a group to select photos in order.

You can also use Ctrl+A to select all photos.

② Click the large green plus sign under Albums and choose New Album to add an album.

The Albums section of the task panel can be opened or closed by clicking the arrow next to the word Albums.

The Album Details panel appears.

③ You can group albums by using the Album Group function, but start with None.

④ Type a name for your album.

⑤ Uncheck Backup/Synchronize until you have a Photoshop.com account (☑ changes to ■).

**Note:** *See Chapter 10 for more about Photoshop.com.*

● Your selected photos appear in the Items box.

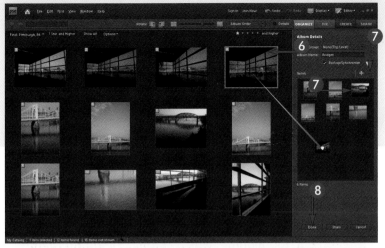

⑥ Click an image and drag it into the Items box to add a photo to an album.

⑦ Click to select an image in the Items box and then click the red minus sign to delete it from the group.

Neither adding nor deleting photos from an album affects their position on the hard drive.

⑧ Click Done.

The new album now appears in the Albums panel.

⑨ Click the album to select it.

The photos you put in the album now appear with a small icon below them to indicate they are in albums.

● To see that icon, select Details (☐ changes to ☑).

● You can edit your album by clicking the Edit icon.

## TIPS

### Did You Know?
You can add photos to an album at any time. Whenever you see a photo that belongs in an album, click it and then drag it to the album. It is automatically put into the album and will appear there whenever that album is opened. Remember you are only creating references to photos and not actually moving any.

### Try This!
You can immediately put any new photos just imported into Photoshop Elements into an album. Simply select all images in that new group of photos, add an album with a name appropriate to that group, and the photos should appear in the Items box. If not, simply select and drag the new pictures into that Item box.

### Smart Albums!
You can create smart albums that automatically add photos to the album. You set up criteria from file names to keywords to camera type in the New Smart Album dialog box, which you access by clicking the Album plus sign (➕). Whenever a photo with those criteria appears in Photoshop Elements, it is automatically included in the smart album.

# USE KEYWORDS
## to tag your images

*Keywords* are words that you add to your photo's metadata (information about the image held in the file). They can be an important way for you to organize and find your pictures because keywords are searchable. Albums are great for creating large groupings of pictures that you can readily access. With keywords and the search function in Organizer, you can go to very specific images depending on how you have used these words for your pictures.

Keywords can be as detailed as you want. You can simply add words to large groups of pictures, which makes this process easier. Or if you want to be able to really find specific images, you can add a lot of very specific keywords to individual pictures.

Regardless of how you use keywords, they are still an important part of Photoshop Elements to understand and use as needed.

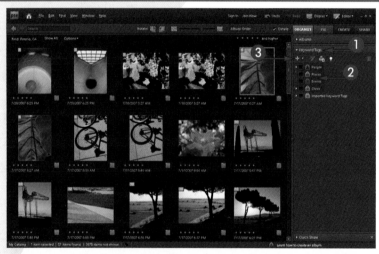

① Click Keyword Tags to open the keyword part of the Organize task panel.

② You can start with the keywords that are listed.

③ Click the large green plus sign under Keyword Tags.

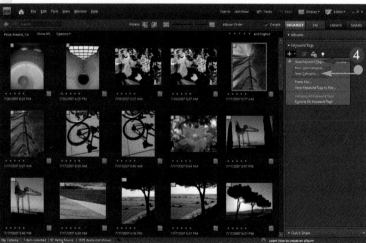

A drop-down menu appears.

● You can choose New Category or New Sub-Category to create your own category for keywords.

④ Choose New Keyword Tag to add a keyword.

The Create Keyword Tag dialog box appears.

⑤ Choose a category.

⑥ Type a name for your keyword tag.

⑦ Choose an icon if desired by clicking Edit Icon.

## 5

**DIFFICULTY LEVEL**

The Edit Keyword Tag Icon dialog box appears.

⑧ Click Import to look for something to use as an icon.

An Explorer window or Open dialog box appears.

⑨ Find a photo that looks interesting, perhaps from the same group of images.

⑩ Click Open to select this photo for your icon.

⑪ Click OK to use this new icon for your keywords.

*Note: It is not required to have an icon for every keyword tag.*

**TIPS**

### Try This!

When all of the task panel controls are open, your interface can get cluttered and confusing. Click the little arrows at the left of the panel category titles to open and close a category of control, such as Albums. Simplify the workspace by closing panel categories you are not using.

### Important!

Pick keywords that help you find your photos. Your keywords will be unique to your type of photography. Adding keywords that others use but do not fit your images will make your searches confusing. Ask yourself, "What do I need to find?" in order to create keywords that work for you and your needs.

### Customize It!

You can add as much or as little information as you want to keyword tags. The Keyword Tags dialog box includes the option to add notes or a specific address for a location. These are not requirements, only options that some photographers will use frequently, others not at all. Use what you need and what works for you.

# USE KEYWORDS
## to tag your images

Keywords are one of those things that many photographers put off. The best time to do keywording is when you first import pictures into Photoshop Elements. At that time, you remember more things about your pictures anyway. It is also easier to add keywords then because all of your pictures are right in front of you.

It is important to understand that you can add keyword tags to one picture and only one picture, to a few pictures, or to hundreds. Keywords allow you to be very specific, down to putting a specific name on something that appears only in one picture. They also allow you to be broader in your approach and put a single word across a whole group of pictures so that you can find that group again. Keywords work across all pictures within Organizer so that you can find pictures throughout Organizer by simply searching for keywords.

- A new keyword tag appears in the category you chose in step 5.

⑫ Select the photos that need this keyword.

   The selected photos have a blue frame around them.

⑬ Click and drag the selected photos onto the tag and they will gain that tag.

   You can click and drag multiple times, with different groups of photos, to add more keyword tags to photos.

- A small keyword tag icon appears below your photos.

⑭ To put a keyword on specific photos, click the tag.

⑮ Drag the tag and drop it on the photo.

   Any new categories used this way appear as new icons below the photo.

16 Find specific images based on your keyword by clicking the check box in front of a specific keyword tag.

17 Click additional tags to narrow your search.

18 To show specific items in an album, click the album before selecting Keyword Tags.

19 To search for images throughout your image files, click Show All first.

20 Type a name in the search box to show photos related to that name quickly.

## TIPS

### Customize It!

Take any existing keyword tag and customize it for your needs. Right-click any keyword tag to get a context-sensitive menu. This allows you to edit your keyword or keyword category, add a new keyword to the category, add a new subcategory, or remove keywords or categories as needed.

### Did You Know?

Photoshop Elements includes a special feature that allows you to find people in your photos for tagging. This is called Find Faces for Tagging and is found in the Keyword Tags category of the task panel. You will see an icon with a person and a yellow tag (📇). Click it and all photos with faces will be highlighted for you.

### Try This!

You can type a list of keywords based on common descriptions of things in your photos. You can then import this list into Photoshop Elements by clicking the green plus sign (➕) under Keyword Tags and then selecting From File. This file must be an XML file. You can save a Word file as an XML file for this purpose.

# CHANGE THE ORGANIZER
## interface as needed

Photoshop Elements has been designed for photographers, and its interface reflects that. However, every photographer has unique needs and ways of working. You can change the way the interface for Organizer looks and consequently acts to customize it for your needs.

The controls for affecting the look of the interface are in the buttons in the top menu bars, such as Album Order or thumbnail size icons, and in the View and Window menus. Do not be afraid to try different looks

for your interface — you can always change back to the original look by re-clicking the button or menu item.

However you set up your interface, it should be something that helps you work more efficiently. Do not simply use something because it is there or because someone else uses it. Be sure that it really does help your work in the program. Working in Elements should be a fun way of interacting with your pictures.

**①** Click the Display button to change your display views.

**②** Click Folder Location view to show a directory tree.

**③** In the Folder Location view, you can click directly on a folder to find photos.

If Elements is not managing pictures in a folder, right-click the folder to add them.

**④** Change your thumbnail size with the thumbnail slider.

DIFFICULTY LEVEL

**5** Click the small arrow next to a right panel category to expand or collapse the panel section.

**6** Click and drag along an interface edge to make it larger or smaller.

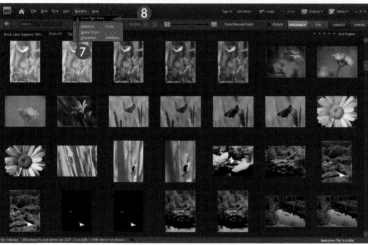

**7** Click Window to change what is seen in the interface.

**8** Click Hide Task Pane to give a large image viewing area; click Show Task Pane to give the normal view.

**TIPS**

### Did You Know?

You can control many features of Photoshop Elements with keyboard commands. These allow you to quickly access controls with just a couple of keystrokes. These keystrokes are listed next to the controls in the menus. For example, you can turn on and off the detail display for thumbnails by using Ctrl+D.

### Try This!

The Timeline in Photoshop Elements can help you find photos by date. This can be turned on in the Windows menu. It works for the entire database, so click the Show All button at the top left of the thumbnails first. Then you can select a specific time, and photos will appear below from that time. You can also drag the left and right sliders to limit the dates to show images.

### Did You Know?

By default, all thumbnails have a small white border around them to make them show up better. Not everyone likes this border, but it can be easily turned off. Go to the View menu and click Show Borders around Thumbnails.

# SET PREFERENCES
## to make Organizer work for you

You can use Photoshop Elements right out of the box and get good results. However, the program has some preferences worth considering that allow you to fine-tune how Elements works with your computer and your needs.

Elements has two sets of preferences, one for the Organizer and one for the Editor. In both cases, they are found at the bottom of the Edit menu. Many of the choices can be left at their default settings, but some can be tweaked to refine how Elements works for you. Many of the settings are self-explanatory. If you are not sure of something and want to try it, go ahead, because all of the settings have a Restore Default Settings button at the bottom of the dialog box. Just reopen Preferences and use this button to go back to the defaults. This section offers some specific options that are especially worth looking at.

① Click Edit to open the Edit menu.

② Click Preferences.

③ Click General.

The Preferences dialog box appears.

④ Adjust Interface Brightness to make the background lighter or darker.

⑤ Choose the order to show images by date (⬤ changes to ◉).

⑥ Select a preferred Date Format (⬤ changes to ◉).

● You can click any category to adjust specific preferences.

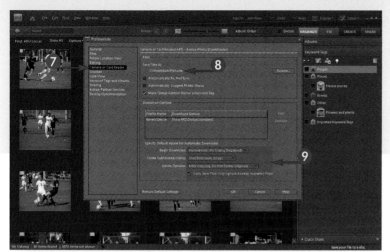

**DIFFICULTY LEVEL**

⑦ Choose Camera or Card Reader.

⑧ Select a default location for your image files as they are copied from your camera or card reader.

⑨ Specify default settings for downloading. The settings shown are a good starting point.

⑩ Click Sharing to set up e-mail with Elements.

⑪ Choose your e-mail program.

⑫ Check Write E-mail captions to catalog to record and save captions (■ changes to ☑).

⑬ Click OK to close the Preferences dialog box.

---

**TIPS**

### Did You Know?

You can have images in a separate location not connected to your computer and still reference them in Organizer. Photoshop Elements keeps a small thumbnail for each of the images so that you can still see them in thumbnail view. You can change the size of these previews in the Files section of Preferences.

### Try This!

Select photos by standard computer selection commands. Ctrl+A selects all photos currently displayed in the organizer. Ctrl+clicking photos selects them one after another. Click one photo, and then Shift+click farther down; all photos in between are selected. You can also deselect a selected photo by Ctrl+clicking it.

### Customize It!

If you use a lot of keywords, you can customize the way they are sorted in Preferences, in the section called Keyword Tags and Albums. You can, for example, change how the keywords are sorted, either alphabetically or manually. You can also choose how the tag icons are used, and you can even adjust how fast or accurate face-tagging is done.

---

## Chapter 1: Organize and Prepare Photos for Processing

# BACK UP YOUR PICTURES
## to protect them

Whenever you read about fires and other disasters destroying people's property, you always read about people wanting to save their photo albums. Photos are important to us in so many ways, whether they are memories of children growing up or artistic visions of a great natural setting.

Digital photos are vulnerable to loss from a hard drive failure — and hard drives do fail. Plus, without a hard copy, you have no other record of the images. By backing them up, you can actually add more security to your pictures than was even possible with

traditional film. It is very easy to back up your photos onto accessory hard drives that plug into your computer. These have come down so much in price that many photographers back up their pictures on more than one.

Backup is so important that Adobe has added special backup features to Photoshop Elements 7, which will be covered in Chapter 10. You should have some backup of your own that you can control and access easily, which is covered here.

An external hard drive is one of the best ways to back up the images on your computer's hard drive.

BACK UP TO AN EXTERNAL HARD DRIVE

1 Click the Display button in the top menu bar.

2 Choose Folder Location.

3 Find a folder you want to duplicate for backup in the folder tree.

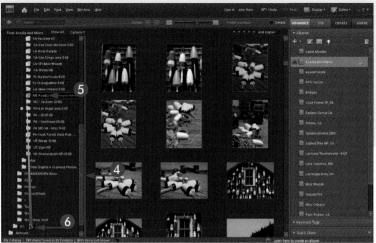

④ If necessary, scroll down to reveal the external hard drive.

⑤ Click the folder you want to duplicate.

⑥ Drag the folder to the external hard drive.

The folder is saved on the external hard drive.

**DIFFICULTY LEVEL**

### Use Backup Software

① With your backup software open, choose the folder or folders you want to back up.

② Click the folder icon to find your folder.

③ Choose the accessory drive for backup.

④ Click the folder icon to select the location for backup.

⑤ Click Run Now to start the backup.

---

**TIPS**

### Did You Know?

Backup software can make your backups easier. Once you set up backup software for specific folders and a specific accessory drive, the software remembers those locations. The next time that you ask it to back up, it simply compares what is in those two locations and adds only what is new.

### Try This!

Small portable hard drives designed for laptops are more expensive than other accessory hard drives. However, they can be handy for accessing your photographs from your laptop or other computer. In addition, you can easily store such a hard drive in a location separate from your main computer, giving you added protection.

### Try This!

When you try to move a folder of pictures on your hard drive to a new drive, Photoshop Elements tells you if those pictures are managed by Organizer or not. If they are not, and you want them included in Photoshop Elements, you can simply right-click the folder and select Add Unmanaged Files to Catalog.

---

# Chapter 2

# Start Adjusting Your Images in Photoshop Elements

A digital camera is an interesting bit of technology. It does a great job of capturing an image from the world, but this image is not necessarily a correct interpretation of that world. A camera is limited by the capabilities of its sensor, by how the camera engineers have designed its internal processing, and its lens. These engineers must create image capture potential for the camera that works for everyone, so consequently it is rarely perfect for anyone.

That is where Photoshop Elements comes in. Most images require you to spend at least a little time tweaking so that they accurately reflect what you originally saw. In this chapter you learn some of the basic steps to get your photos looking more the way you expect a photograph to look. This chapter also reflects a workflow from start to finish that can be used as you work on your pictures. A few of the steps, such as setting blacks and whites, adjusting midtones, and color correction, are important steps for any photograph.

# Top 100

# Open pictures and
# USE SAVE AS

To start the process of working on photos in Photoshop Elements, you need to get a picture into the Editor workspace of Photoshop Elements. You can work with Organizer or you can get images directly into Editor from the File menu there. The advantage of working with Organizer is that you have access to lots of pictures at once. If you are working with a specific picture and you know exactly where it is, opening the picture directly in Editor can be easier.

Many photographers worry about adversely affecting an image and so are very cautious about working on it. If you immediately save any picture as a new file when it is opened into Photoshop Elements, you are protecting your original image file. This can free you to do the needed work on your image without worrying about permanently damaging it. You cannot damage your original because you are not working on it at this point.

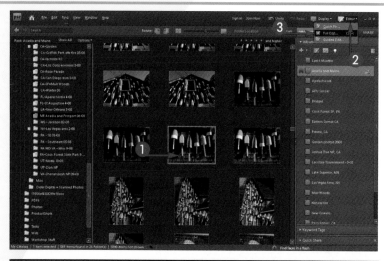

① Click a photo to select it.

② Click the Editor icon.

③ Select Full Edit.

The photo appears in Editor.

④ Click File.

⑤ Select Save As.

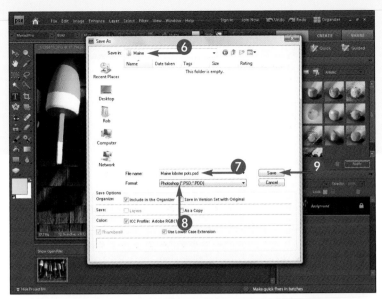

The Save As dialog box appears.

**6** Choose a location to save your photos.

**7** Give your photo a name that makes sense to you.

**8** Choose either Photoshop (.psd) or TIFF (.tif) for format.

**9** Click Save.

If you chose Photoshop in step 8, your photo is saved.

If you chose TIFF in step 8, the TIFF options dialog box appears.

**10** Choose None ( changes to ) for image compression, although LZW can be used if your photos will be opened only in Elements.

**11** Leave the lower radio buttons and check boxes at the default settings.

**12** Click OK.

## Try This!

You can open photos directly from Editor. Click File and then choose Open. This takes you to the Open dialog box. Navigate to where your digital photos are kept, and then find the folder and the image. When you click a photo once to select it, a preview appears. Click Open to open it in Editor.

## Did You Know?

Photographers should save images in Photoshop, TIFF, and JPEG formats. JPEG should not be used as a working file format, that is, one that you use to work on images while you are in Editor. JPEG is a compression file format and should be used only for archiving images when you need to keep file sizes small or for e-mail and Web purposes. The Photoshop format is ideal because it allows you to do all kinds of work on a picture and save everything, including layers, when you save the file. The TIFF format is a good one when you need to open pictures in other programs, such as in Word or Publisher. Both Photoshop and TIFF allow you to open, adjust, and save an image as much as you want without quality loss because of the format.

# MAKE THE EDITOR INTERFACE
## your own

The Editor interface of Photoshop Elements is very adaptable. Most photographers find it helpful to make some adjustments to that interface so that the program works better for you. For some reason, Adobe has decided to put Effects in the right side palette bin as a default and not Undo History. Although many photographers use Effects, almost all photographers use Undo History.

In this task, you learn to create an efficient workspace for most photographers. You also learn

how to add or subtract palettes from the interface so you can do your own customization.

You can always turn on or off parts of the interface by checking items in the Window menu. Do not be afraid to turn off parts of the interface that you do not use or turn on something that seems useful for your purposes even if it is not included here. You can also reset the interface in the Window menu by checking Reset Palette Locations.

① Click the double arrows at the right of Effects to get a drop-down menu.

② Click Place in Palette Bin when Closed to uncheck it.

③ Click the Effects bar.

④ Drag the Effects palette out of the palette bin.

⑤ Click the X at the upper right to close the palette.

6  Click Window.

7  Select Undo History in the menu.

● The Undo History palette appears.

8  Click the More button.

9  Check Place in Palette Bin when Closed.

10  Click the X to close the palette and send it to the palette bin under Layers.

Undo History is now locked to the palette bin.

## TIPS

### Try This!
The Project Bin at the bottom of the interface shows the active images in Photoshop Elements, whether there is one or more. If you want more working space, you can always hide this panel. Simply click Hide Project Bin at the bottom left. To bring the bin back, click Show Project Bin that appears in the same place.

### Try This!
You can make the Undo History palette larger or smaller in the palette bin. Click and drag the separating line between it and the Layers palette; the cursor changes to a small double arrow when you are over the right spot. You can also make your palette bin larger or smaller by clicking and dragging the left edge.

### Did You Know?
The dark gray interface of Photoshop Elements was chosen very deliberately by Adobe. This color sets pictures off well and makes them the stars of the interface. In addition, the neutral color does not compete with or affect our perception of colors in a photograph.

# SET PREFERENCES
## to make Editor work for you

Just as in the Organizer (see task #7), Editor has preferences that you can set to make the program run more efficiently with the computer. They are in the same place in the menu as they were in Organizer, under the Edit menu, down at the bottom. You could use all of the defaults in these preferences and still work fine with Photoshop Elements. Adobe has put a lot of thought into the defaults, so they do work. However, a lot of them are chosen based on

what most people might do, not necessarily what you would do.

In Preferences, you can choose to affect all sorts of things, from how files are saved to performance of Photoshop Elements with your computer to plug-ins and more. Most of the options are fairly self-explanatory, and if you are not sure what they do, you can always try them and then reset everything later.

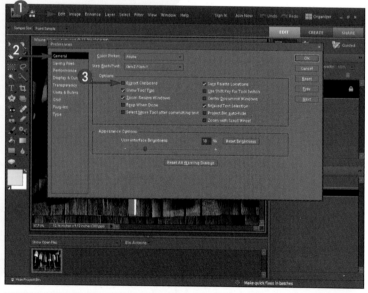

1 Click Edit and then Preferences to open the Preferences dialog box.

2 Choose a set of preferences from the left list; this task begins with General.

Most of General can be left at the defaults.

3 Uncheck Export Clipboard to keep the Clipboard empty except when you want something copied to it (☑ changes to ■).

4 Click Saving Files.

5 From the On First Save drop-down menu, select Save Over Current File for efficient work or Always Ask if you want to be extra safe.

The defaults work well for the rest of the options.

6 Click Performance.

7 Set memory usage to the highest number in the Ideal Range unless you have less than 1GB of RAM.

8 Check any accessory drives for Scratch Disks to ensure you have scratch space (■ changes to ☑).

**DIFFICULTY LEVEL**

9 Click Display & Cursors.

10 Choose how your brush will display with painting cursors (◉ changes to ◉).

You can keep the defaults to start, but change this later if you prefer a precise cursor, for example.

11 Check Show Crosshair in Brush Tip to show the center of a working brush (■ changes to ☑).

12 Click OK to close the Preferences dialog box.

---

**TIPS**

### Did You Know?

When Photoshop Elements runs out of RAM or "thinking space," it needs someplace to work, and so it uses space on a hard drive. This is called *scratch space,* and the drive being used is the *scratch drive.* It can be helpful to have more than one drive designated for scratch space so that Photoshop Elements never runs out of room to think.

### More Options!

Color Settings are a group of preferences that have their own separate settings. They are accessed in the Edit menu, too. You will do okay with these set at the defaults, but you get more capabilities and options for how color can be adjusted if you select Always Optimize for Printing. This gives you what is called the Adobe RGB color space.

### Did You Know?

A color space is something a computer uses to describe how colors are rendered. A common color space for JPEG files is sRGB, which works fine for many images but is a smaller color space than Adobe RGB. Adobe RGB gives more flexibility and options when you are adjusting color and tonality.

# EXPERIMENT TO LEARN
## more about controls

Many photographers get very cautions when working on pictures in Photoshop Elements. That is actually not the best way to work. An experimental approach shows you what controls do or do not do to a picture very quickly, whereas a more cautious approach may limit you because you do not see the possibilities.

Sometimes it is hard to remember what all the controls are in Photoshop Elements. You do not have to remember all of the controls perfectly. In fact, a

great way of learning the program is simply to try them out. Experiment. See what controls do or do not do to pictures. Then simply use Ctrl+Z to undo anything that you have done.

As you see in task #13, you cannot really hurt your pictures. Experimenting frees you to look for possibilities so that you can get the most out of your pictures.

EXPERIMENT WITH LEVELS

① Click Enhance.

② Select Adjust Lighting.

③ Choose Levels.

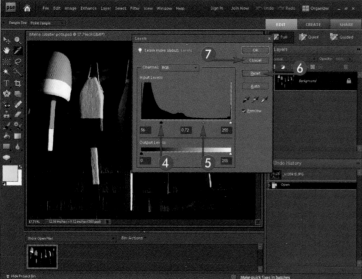

The Levels dialog box opens.

④ Click the black slider and move it to the right.

⑤ Click the gray slider and move it to the right.

This makes the photo darker.

⑥ Click Reset to reset the sliders at any time.

⑦ Click Cancel.

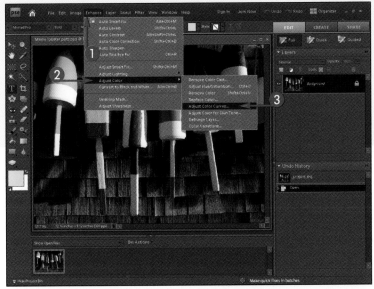

EXPERIMENT WITH COLOR
CURVES

1. Click Enhance.

2. Select Adjust Color.

3. Click Adjust Color
Curves.

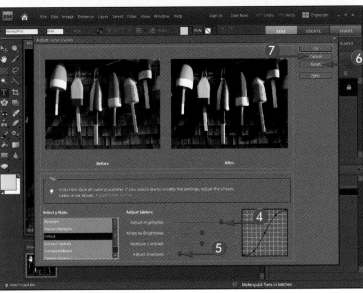

The Adjust Color Curves dialog
box appears.

4. Click and drag the Adjust
Highlights slider far to the right.

5. Click and drag the Adjust
Shadows slider far to the left.

The image gets very contrasty.

6. Click Reset at any time.

7. Click Cancel.

## TIPS

### Did You Know?

Dialog boxes are not always in the
best places when they open.
Frequently, they cover up
important parts of the picture. You
can easily move the dialog box to a
different location by clicking the
top bar of the dialog box and then
dragging the whole thing to a new
place on your screen.

### Test It!

You can quickly see the before and
after versions of your picture when
you are making adjustments. Also,
all dialog boxes for adjustments
include a small check box for
something called Preview. Check
this box on and off to see what the
picture looks like with and without
the adjustments. Preview on shows
you what the adjustments look like.

### Get Help!

Dialog boxes in Photoshop
Elements frequently include a
Learn About link that refers
specifically to the control you are
working with. This is a great
resource. Simply click the blue
word that describes the function of
your dialog box and you
immediately go to a help page
explaining it.

# YOU CANNOT HURT
## your pictures

Another reason many photographers get very cautious when working on pictures in Photoshop Elements is that they are afraid of hurting their images. You cannot really hurt your pictures. This is an important thing to keep in mind because it frees you to work more confidently with your pictures.

As long as you have done a Save As for your original image (see task #9), you cannot hurt the original image because you are now working on a copy. And

as you work, you can always undo everything that you have already done. As long as you do not save what you have done, there is no change made to the file you are working on except within Photoshop Elements. The Undo History palette gives you even more options to back up on your adjustments. Knowing all of this can help you experiment without restraint to really discover possibilities for your image.

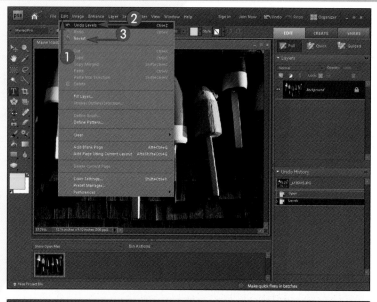

### REVERSE ADJUSTMENTS

**1** Click Edit.

**2** Select Undo Levels.

*Note: Alternately, use Ctrl+Z.*

**3** Select Revert to go back to the last saved version of the open file.

### RESET A DIALOG BOX

**1** Press and hold the Alt key and the Cancel button changes to Reset.

**2** Click Reset.

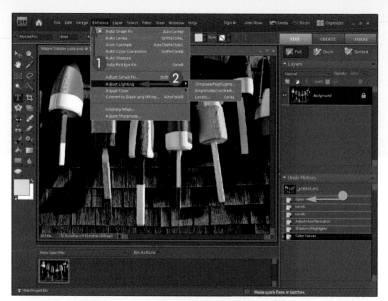

**#13**

**DIFFICULTY LEVEL**

① Click Enhance.

② Randomly make some adjustments from Adjust Lighting and Adjust Color. You do not have to know what you are doing.

● All adjustments appear in the Undo History palette.

③ Click any adjustment in the Undo History palette to go back to an earlier adjustment.

*Note: You can also keep pressing Ctrl+Z to back up in this palette.*

**TIPS**

### Try This!

Set your Undo History palette for more or fewer adjustment steps or states by clicking Edit, Preferences, and then Performance (see task #11). When you are just doing a few things on the picture, having a lot of history states is not important. In fact, having more states can slow down your program as it struggles to remember all of them. But as you advance in your work within Photoshop Elements, you will find that some changes you will make to an image will quickly go through the History palette. If you have more RAM, you can typically add more history states.

### Caution!

There is one way that you can lose your ability to back up from adjustments. If you make a lot of adjustments to a picture and then save and close it, you have now locked those adjustments to the picture. Save your photo as you go, but only when you are sure that your adjustments are okay. Later in this book (see task #24), you learn how to make nondestructive adjustments that even allow you to close and save an image with those changes intact and still adjustable.

# CROP YOUR PHOTOS
## for tighter shots

A common problem for photographers is getting too much in a picture. Sometimes this comes from not being able to get close enough to the subject. Other times it comes from an excitement about the subject when seen in person that does not quite translate to the actual photograph.

Another challenge for photographers is when unwanted stuff starts creeping into the edges of a picture. That can make the photograph less than its best and even distinctly unappealing.

Luckily, Photoshop Elements makes this easy to fix. You can simply crop your picture down to the essential elements of that image. *Cropping* is simply cutting off parts of the picture so that you can reveal the real image obscured by those extra parts. Cropping to strengthen an image and get rid of junk is best done early on in the process. Cropping to a specific size should be done after you have adjusted your photograph optimally.

**①** Click the Crop tool in the toolbox at the left.

**②** Delete any numbers in the Width, Height, or Resolution boxes.

**③** Click a corner of the area you want to keep.

**④** Drag your cursor to the opposite corner of the area.

**5** Click and drag any corner of the crop box to resize it.

**6** Click and drag any edge to resize.

**7** Click the green check mark to complete the crop.

● The red circle removes the crop box.

**DIFFICULTY LEVEL**

The cropped image now appears in the work area at the same pixel size, but with less image because of the crop.

*Note: You can resize this to fill the work area by pressing Ctrl+0.*

**TIPS**

### Try This!

If the Crop tool is not cooperating, you can reset it easily. This is true for all tools. Just above the work area and the toolbox is a toolbar of options for the tool that you are working with. At the far left is a small down-facing arrow. Click that to see options for resetting this tool or all tools. Click Reset Tool.

### Try This!

You do not have to use the green check mark to finish your crop. Sometimes it is not very efficient to go searching for that green check mark. You can use the keyboard and simply press Enter. Or you can use your mouse and double-click inside the box to complete the crop.

### Did You Know?

Cropping out the junk early on in the photograph actually helps as you process the image in Photoshop Elements. Whenever you make any adjustment, Elements is looking at the entire picture. Stuff in the picture that really does not belong there can throw off your adjustment.

# FIX AND ROTATE
## crooked pictures

It is so easy to get crooked pictures. Even the pros get them. What happens is that the photographer is so excited by the scene or the action within that scene that he or she does not pay strict attention to the horizon.

Then when the photographer is back in front of the computer, he or she notices that the horizon is crooked. This can be a problem because people do notice crooked horizons. And even if they do not, the photographer usually does and is disappointed in that lack of horizontal. Of course, pictures can have crooked verticals, too, but the corrections are the same.

Photoshop Elements makes it very easy to straighten a horizon. You can do it in a couple of ways. What method to use really depends a lot on the photograph, the degree of crookedness, and your workflow needs.

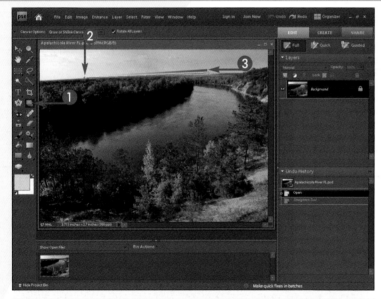

**USE THE STRAIGHTEN TOOL**

1. Click the Straighten tool in the toolbox at the left, just below the Crop tool.

2. Click one side of the crooked horizon.

3. Drag and release the mouse button when you have created a line across the crooked horizon.

Photoshop Elements straightens the horizon, which makes the picture look crooked in the work area.

4. Click the Crop tool.

5. Crop the key part of the photo to remove awkward corners.

6. Click the green check mark to finish.

38

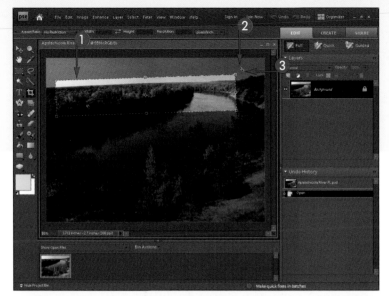

**1** Make a narrow crop selection near the horizon with the Crop tool.

**2** Position your cursor outside the bounding box until it turns into a curved, two-headed arrow.

**3** Click and drag to rotate the bounding box so an edge is parallel to the horizon.

**4** Expand the crop box until it covers the correct parts of the photo.

**5** Click the green check mark to finish.

## TIPS

### Try This!

Extreme angles can be fun. Try rotating the crop box to odd and unusual angles and see what happens to the photo. Sometimes you will find very interesting and stimulating results. But other times you will get nothing. Keep trying!

### Did You Know?

There is a Photoshop joke that applies to Elements, too. How many Elements experts does it take to screw in a light bulb? 51 — one person to screw in the bulb and fifty to describe another way to do it. Photoshop and Photoshop Elements are very powerful and flexible. Use the tools that work for you and ignore people who tell you that you are doing it all wrong. You have to find your own way through the program. This can take some work and time, but it is well worth it when you can work more efficiently.

# USE GUIDED EDIT
## to help you learn the program

A quick and easy way of getting into working on your images in Photoshop Elements is to use the Guided Edit feature of the program. This feature guides you through working on an image, plus it gives you a good idea about how Photoshop Elements works.

This truly is a guided part of Photoshop Elements. You get a lot of different options about how you might adjust the picture, but no controls are visible to distract you. You are thinking only about what needs

to be done to a photograph. Guided Edit does not cover everything in Photoshop Elements but it does give a good overview of the program. Simply click any option in Guided Edit to be taken to the actual control that you need as well as instructions on how to use it. There are 19 different controls here with very specific helps on how to use them. The steps that follow show two as examples.

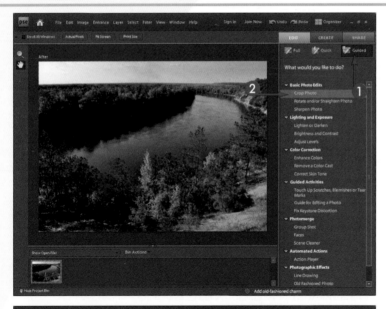

### USE CROP PHOTO

① Click the Guided tab below and to the right of the orange Edit tab.

A new panel appears.

② Click Crop Photo.

The Crop tool is selected, a crop box is applied, and instructions appear in the right panel.

③ Click the crop box edges to revise your crop.

④ Click Done when you are finished.

**DIFFICULTY LEVEL**

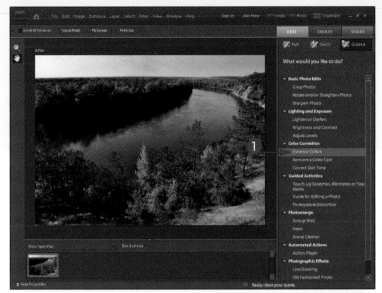

**1** Click Enhance Colors.

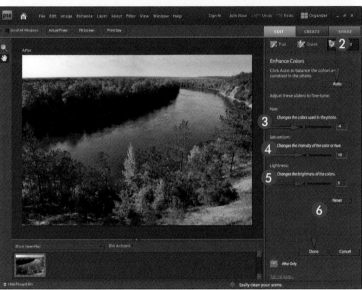

**2** Try clicking Auto if your colors seem off.

**3** Drag the Hue slider to change the color of the colors.

**4** Drag the Saturation slider to change the intensity of the colors.

**5** Drag the Lightness slider to change the brightness of colors.

**6** Click Done when you are finished.

---

TIPS

### Caution!
Several controls in the Guided Edit panel can be easily and quickly overdone, causing you problems when you want to print your photo or use it in other ways. Be very careful with how strongly you use the brightness and contrast, sharpening, and saturation slide controls. There are no warnings about this in the panel.

### Try This!
When using the Guided Edit panel, you may find that you inadvertently get adjustments you thought you canceled. That is not a problem. There is no harm here, but do not try to correct the adjustment while still in the Guided Edit panel. Just go to Full Edit and use your Undo History palette.

### Remember This!
Almost all of the panels in Guided Edit have a Reset button. This can be a real help for you. On some of the panels, it is easy to get going quickly and over-adjust certain controls. It can be hard and confusing to try to readjust them back to zero. Instead, just use the Reset button.

# SET BLACKS AND WHITES
## with Levels

A very important part of any photograph is how the pure black and pure white elements of the image are adjusted. Many cameras do not give a pure black in the image files. Camera designers recognize that black needs can vary depending on the type of photography, so they keep this adjustment minimal with the expectation that the photographer should adjust that.

For most pictures, you want a pure black and a pure white somewhere in the picture. Ansel Adams made

this a key point of working in the darkroom, and the needs of a digital color photograph are no different. Without a proper black and white, the picture will not have the best color, the best contrast, or the best overall look. Photographers are often amazed at how much even adjusting the blacks and whites affects the look of the picture without doing anything else. Usually an image requires other adjustments, but this is a good starting point for any photograph.

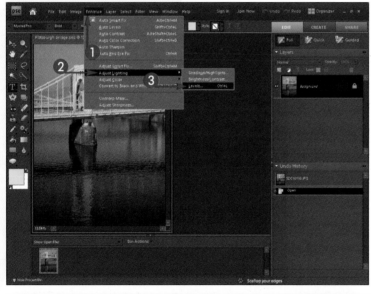

1. Click Enhance.
2. Select Adjust Lighting.
3. Select Levels.

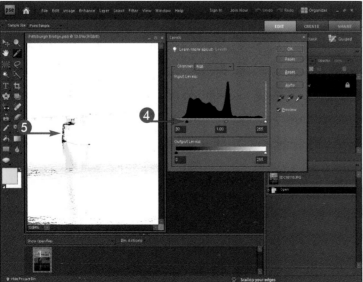

The Levels dialog box appears.

4. Press the Alt key as you move the black slider under the graph, or *histogram*.

   A threshold screen appears showing when pure black appears in the photo.

5. Move the slider until at least something black shows.

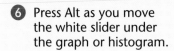

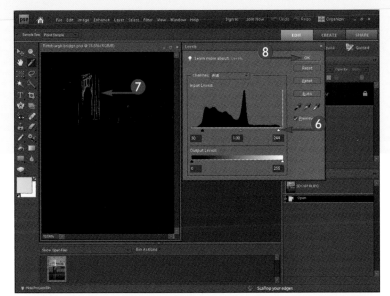

**6** Press Alt as you move the white slider under the graph or histogram.

A threshold screen appears showing when pure white appears in the photo.

**7** Move the slider until at least something shows.

White is very sensitive, so you can stop when colors appear.

**8** Click OK when done.

**#17**

**DIFFICULTY LEVEL**

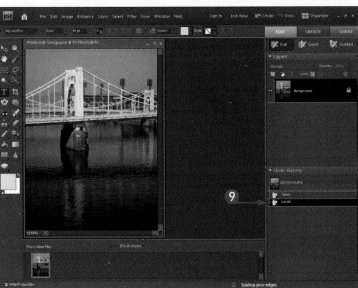

The image in the work area now has better color and contrast.

**9** Click between Open and Levels in Undo History to see the differences.

### Did You Know?

Adjusting the blacks, which refers to all areas of black, is very subjective. Some photographers want a very strong and large area of black within their photograph. Others prefer just a few blacks showing up in the threshold screen. Whites are not so subjective. You have to be very careful not to over-brighten them.

### Caution!

Foggy days do not have blacks. If you try to get blacks showing up in the threshold screen on such an image, the picture will look harsh and unappealing. Because setting up blacks is subjective, you really have to pay attention to your photograph and its needs, as well as your interpretation of the scene.

### More Options!

You may find that some pictures do not seem to have a pure black. All that shows up in the threshold screen is a color. Strongly colored pictures act like this. Do not try to get a pure black, but be sure that you are getting a strong color at least somewhere. That color shows that a channel has been maxed out.

# ADJUST YOUR MIDTONES
## with Levels

When you set blacks properly, you often find your photo is too dark. It is not actually the whole photo that is too dark, but the *midtones*, the tonalities between black and white.

In fact, these middle tonalities are extremely important to your photograph. They affect the overall brightness of the image, the colors of the photo, and the ability of a viewer to see detail within the picture. Some photographers refer to brightening the

midtones as "opening up" certain tonalities. This is a good way to look at it. You are trying to open up certain parts of the picture so that they can be better seen by the viewer.

This is a very subjective adjustment. There is no right or wrong. You have to look at your picture and decide what is the right interpretation for the subject and for how you saw it.

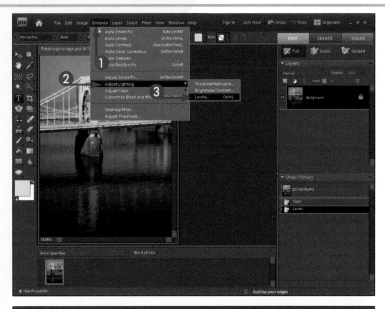

① Click Enhance.

② Select Adjust Lighting.

③ Select Levels.

The Levels dialog box appears.

④ Move the middle slider left to brighten the photo.

⑤ Move the middle slider right to darken it.

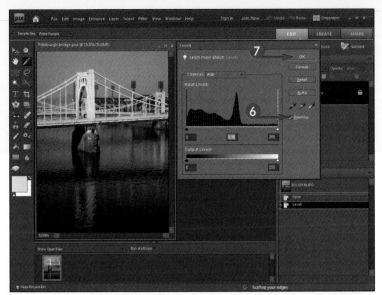

**6** Click the Preview check box to turn the adjustment on and off (☐ changes to ☑).

This allows you to better see what is happening in the photo.

**7** Click OK when done.

**DIFFICULTY LEVEL**

The image in your work area now has more open midtones and color.

**8** Click between Open, Levels, and Levels in Undo History to see the differences.

The two Levels make it easy to see the different adjustments.

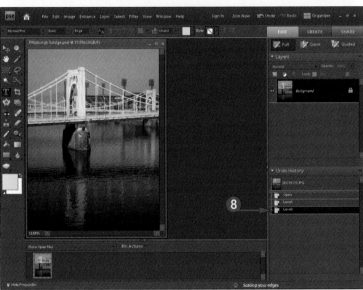

**TIPS**

### Did You Know?
By separating these adjustments into two uses of Levels, you can more easily see the adjustments and make corrections to them. This step-by-step approach also keeps the steps separate in the Undo History palette. That makes it easier for you to find exactly where a particular adjustment is affecting your picture.

### Did You Know?
The graph in Levels is called a *histogram*, which is a chart of the brightness values of the pixels in your photograph. As you adjust Levels, you will see small gaps or white lines appear in the histogram. Small gaps are not a problem.

### Important!
The middle slider in Levels is a midtones slider, but it actually affects more than just the very middle tones. As you work in Elements, you will start noticing differences between the dark tones with details, middle tones, and bright tones with detail.

# ADJUST YOUR MIDTONES
## with Color Curves

Another way of adjusting midtones is to use Color Curves. Do not be misled by this name. Although the Color Curves adjustment does affect color to a degree, it really is a way of affecting tonalities.

The midtones slider in Levels affects midtones separately from blacks and whites, with most of the adjustment near the middle tones. You cannot adjust darker tones separately from lighter tones, for example.

Color Curves allows you to separate these adjustments. This gives you more control over the whole range of tones in your picture between the blacks and the whites. This can allow you to open up dark areas, while keeping bright areas at their original darkness for example. This is important because the camera often captures tonalities in a scene far differently than the way we see them with our eyes. Color Curves gives us one way of adjusting for that.

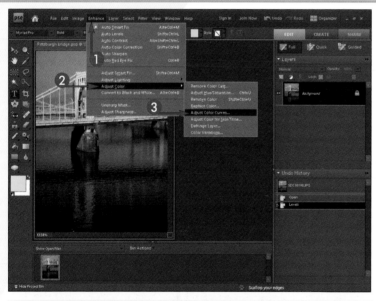

1 Click Enhance.

2 Select Adjust Color.

3 Select Adjust Color Curves.

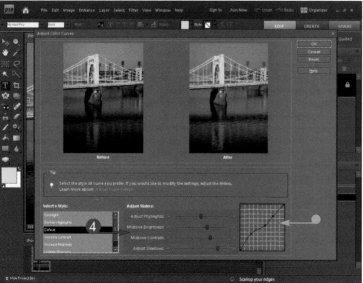

The Adjust Color Curves dialog box appears.

4 Move the parametric sliders to adjust specific tones in your photo.

You can move the sliders to the right to make tones brighter or contrast higher.

You can move the sliders to the left to make tones darker or contrast less.

● The graph, which shows curves for the adjustments, changes as you move the sliders, but you do not have to know anything about it to use this tool.

**⑤** Select a style at the left side in order to create adjustments semi-automatically based on the short descriptions there.

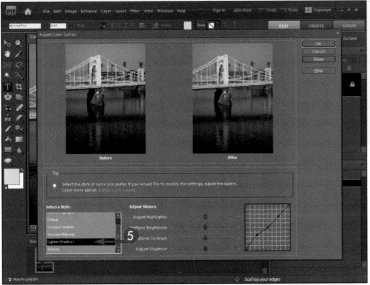

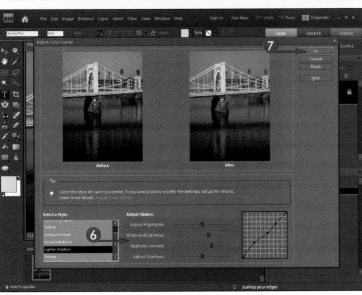

**⑥** Click and adjust the parametric sliders as needed to tweak the style.

**⑦** Click OK when done.

# TIPS

## Did You Know?

The sliders in Color Curves are called parametric sliders because they have very specific parameters that they affect. They include making highlights brighter or darker, changing the brightness or darkness as well as the contrast of middle tones, and making shadows brighter or darker.

## Did You Know?

Color Curves are named after an important adjustment in Photoshop called Curves. As you adjust individual tonalities within a picture, such as highlights separately from shadows, the graph starts creating curves in its main line, thus the name Curves. The graph actually represents black at the bottom left and white at the top right.

## Try This!

Quick adjustments are better than slow adjustments. Many photographers try to make small adjustments when working in Photoshop Elements. It is actually easier to see the difference between a good and a bad adjustment if you make the adjustments quickly.

# QUICKLY ADJUST
## dark shadows and bright highlights

One challenge that consistently faces photographers is a scene that has very bright highlights, or bright areas, and very dark shadows, or dark areas, all within the photo you want to take. The camera then has trouble balancing the brightness throughout the picture. You can see the shadows and highlights just fine, but the camera cannot see the way that you do.

Photoshop Elements can help with this with an adjustment control called Shadows/Highlights. This control has been designed to search out the very darkest parts of the picture and then adjust them while limiting the adjustment to those tones. It has also been designed to find the very brightest parts of the picture and then limit any adjustments to them as well. It is a very handy control to know about, but it should be used after you adjust blacks and whites as well as midtones.

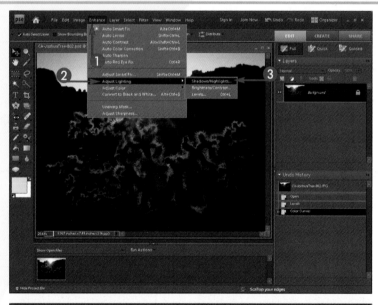

① Click Enhance.

② Select Adjust Lighting.

③ Select Shadows/Highlights.

The Shadows/Highlights dialog box appears.

④ Click the Lighten Shadows slider and move it to the right to brighten your shadows.

It is important to carefully do these adjustments one at a time to see the effects on the appearance of the photograph.

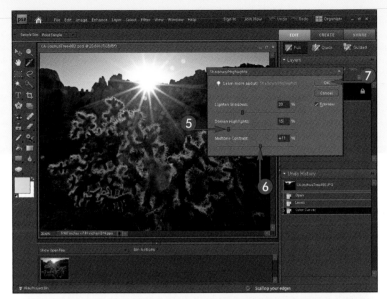

**5** Click the Darken Highlights slider and move it to the right to make your highlights have more color and detail.

**6** Click the Midtone Contrast slider and move it to the right or left to make the picture look more natural.

**7** Click OK to finish.

**DIFFICULTY LEVEL**

The adjusted photo now appears in the central work area of Photoshop Elements.

**8** Click different lines, called *states*, of Undo History to see if the adjustments are doing what you want done to your image.

**TIPS**

### Important!
Shadows/Highlights is no magic bullet — it cannot cure all contrast problems in a photograph. Your picture must have detail to work with in the dark and light areas. Shadows/Highlights cannot add detail that the camera did not originally capture.

### Did You Know?
Noise creates a sand-like pattern in a picture and can be very annoying. It is rarely noticeable in bright areas with normal exposures. However, it lurks hidden in the dark areas of the picture. When dark areas are much brightened with Shadows/Highlights, noise often becomes more obvious. See task #31 for more about noise.

### Caution!
The Shadows/Highlights control is easy to overdo. Watch your picture. Do not simply adjust it so you can see lots of detail in shadows or more detailed highlights. That can result in unnatural-looking images. Make your adjustments so that your picture looks like it really was taken on this planet!

# CORRECT COLOR
## to remove color casts

Color casts are those slight overall colors that seem to permeate the picture. They make neutral colors not neutral, and they can hurt the appearance of colors so the colors are no longer accurate to the way we saw them. They can cause problems for your subject and your rendition of the scene.

Color casts come from all sorts of things, from fluorescent lights to blue skies to improper white balance — all fill a scene with colors that compromise

the look of an image. They used to be a very big problem with film, but they are reduced with digital because of the white balance control. White balance works to reduce color casts due to the color of light. This helps, but you can still get a picture with color casts that need to be corrected. A consistent problem with a lot of cameras is that auto white balance often gives a slight cold or blue cast to the picture, which can affect skin tones and make them look less attractive.

### Remove a Color Cast
1. Click Enhance.
2. Select Adjust Color.
3. Select Remove Color Cast.

The Remove Color Cast dialog box appears.

4. Position your cursor over the photo; the cursor turns into an eyedropper.

5. Click the eyedropper on something that should be neutral in color — a white, gray, or black.

   Color casts are removed, but the first click might not work.

6. Click Reset if the colors are not right.

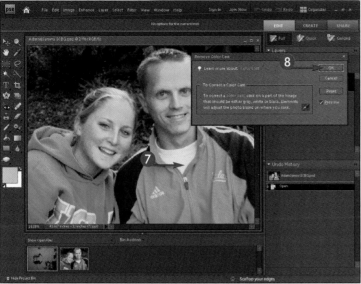

**7** Keep clicking different tones that should be neutral, clicking Reset if the colors are bad, until you get a good color balance.

**8** Click OK to finish.

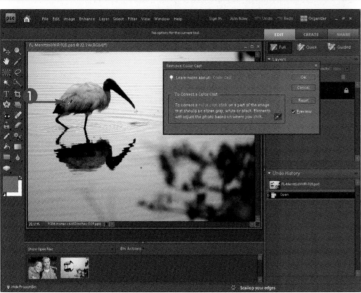

## REMOVE ANOTHER COLOR CAST

This technique works for more than people photographs.

**1** With the Remove Color Cast dialog box open, click different tones in the photo until the color is corrected.

## TIPS

### Did You Know?
The Levels dialog box has three eyedroppers on the right side. The black and white eyedroppers affect blacks and whites, but they are very heavy-handed and not as effective as using the Levels sliders. The middle eyedropper is in fact the same eyedropper as the one used in Remove Color Cast.

### Did You Know?
You can further adjust the color of skin tones by going to Adjust Color for Skin Tone in Enhance and then clicking Adjust Color. In this control, you click the skin of a person and Elements adjusts the color of the whole picture to make the skin look better. You can further tweak this with some sliders.

### Try This!
As you click around in your photograph, you will often find the picture changes to some rather odd colors. That is not a problem because you can simply click the Reset button. However, you may sometimes find these colors are interesting. You can even try clicking colors in the picture just to see what happens.

# ENHANCE COLOR
## with Hue/Saturation

When photographers discover that they can increase *saturation*, or the color intensity, of the picture with Hue/Saturation, they sometimes get too excited about saturation. The saturation control in Hue/Saturation can very quickly go from enhancing colors to making them look garish.

Although you can adjust the overall colors with Saturation, be careful that you do not overdo it. An adjustment of ten points or so is usually plenty. The

best way to adjust the saturation in a picture is to adjust individual colors. Your camera does not capture colors equally, so this is a way of getting better color with any photograph.

Hue/Saturation also allows you to adjust the color of the color, or its *hue*. Using the techniques described here, you can, for example, correct the hue of a flower or change the color of someone's jacket by changing the Hue slider.

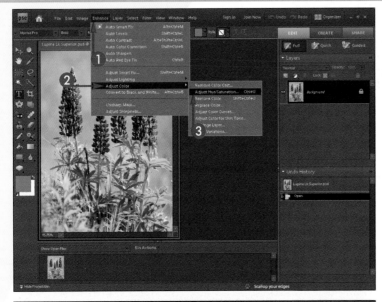

① Click Enhance.

② Select Adjust Color.

③ Select Adjust Hue/Saturation.

The Hue/Saturation dialog box appears.

④ Click the Edit drop-down menu.

⑤ Click the first color you want to adjust.

The Edit menu now changes to the color you have selected, and Photoshop Elements restricts adjustments to that color.

**6** Click and drag the Saturation slider to the right to increase saturation.

**7** If needed, click and drag the Hue slider left or right to change the hue of the color.

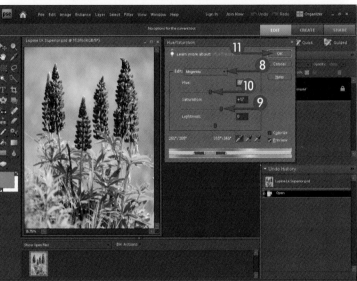

**8** Click in the Edit drop-down menu again to pick a new color.

**9** Click and drag the Saturation slider to the right to increase this color's saturation.

**10** Click and drag the Hue slider if needed.

**11** Click OK to finish.

## TIPS

### Try This!
Use your cursor to click in the photo to define color for Hue/Saturation. Once you have selected a color in the Edit menu, simply position your cursor over the picture and it turns into an eyedropper. Click the color in the photo and that color will be more carefully chosen within Hue/Saturation for the control.

### Did You Know?
Lightness looks like it should be a good control in Hue/Saturation. Unfortunately it is not. It tends to dull colors instead of simply making them lighter or darker. It is okay to use in small amounts, but you will find that your colors do not look their best if you try to use it more than that.

### Caution!
Be wary of over-saturating your pictures. This control quickly locks up your colors and makes them look garish if you are not careful. Make your adjustments quickly so that you can see how different the colors are changing and so that your eye does not get used to the gradual color changes.

# Use Quick Edit to
# WORK FAST

Sometimes you have some pictures that you want to work on very quickly. You may have promised some prints to a friend or maybe you just need to get them ready for presentation. Although all of the controls that you have seen in this chapter work well, one challenge is that you have to open up each control individually. That takes time.

In Photoshop Elements Quick Edit, you gain a number of adjustments all in one place that do not need to be

opened separately. These adjustments are not as controllable or as flexible as Photoshop Elements' main controls, but they do work when you need to process pictures quickly. Quick Edit also includes some auto controls. These are also helpful for fast adjustments, but they can at times take you in the wrong directions for your picture because they are based on formulas instead of what your picture actually looks like.

① Click the Quick Edit tab.

Examine the General Fixes area.

● If you need to fix red-eye problems, click that Auto button.

Smart Fix may or may not help your photo.

If you do not like any adjustment, you can press Ctrl+Z to undo it.

② Click the left arrow of a panel category to close that area when not needed.

③ Click the Levels and Contrast Auto buttons.

④ Adjust the Lighting sliders to make your photo gain the right tonalities.

⑤ Click the green check mark to okay the adjustments or the red circle to remove them.

**6** Click the Color Auto button to see if it helps the photo.

**7** Adjust overall color saturation as needed.

**8** Adjust Temperature and Tint to affect color casts and the warmth of a photo.

# 23

DIFFICULTY LEVEL

**9** Open Sharpen by clicking the small arrow at the left of the category name.

**10** Click the Sharpen Auto button.

**11** Adjust Amount to give more or less sharpening.

**12** Click the specialized Touch Up tools, including red-eye brush, teeth whitening brush, sky brush, and high-contrast black-and-white, as appropriate.

## Try This!

Try the auto controls, but if they do not work, immediately use Ctrl+Z. Auto controls are based on formulas developed by the Photoshop Elements designers. They can work, but they are also somewhat arbitrary because a designer cannot know every person's photos.

## Did You Know?

Smart Fix is a useful adjustment when the photo looks a bit off right from the start. For many photos, however, you will find that using Levels and Contrast Auto buttons gives better results. You can use Levels alone or add Contrast — this gives you more options and control.

## Try This!

Quick Fix can also be used for a starting point for other adjustments. You do not have to make this an either/or question, that is, use Full Edit or Quick Edit. Use Quick Edit to start the process and then refine your adjustments in Full Edit. If you do this, do not use the Sharpen panel area.

# 3

# Work with RAW Photos in Photoshop Elements

The RAW format available in all digital SLRs is a distinct choice from JPEG shooting. Some advanced compact digital cameras also have the RAW format. The RAW and JPEG issue is not an arbitrary quality issue, though some people try to make it so. You can get outstanding results from digital photos whether they are shot in JPEG or RAW.

RAW offers some special benefits that you may want to consider, and these benefits can make RAW a good choice for photography. *RAW* is a file that maximizes the information that comes

from your sensor. It includes a great deal more tone and color steps than is possible with JPEG. This gives you a lot more flexibility in processing an image before you start to see problems with tones or colors. You can do a lot of things with a JPEG image, but you can do more with a RAW file.

RAW files allow you to dig more detail out of bright areas in a picture, unearth more tones in dark areas, and ensure better gradations when adjusting smooth gradients like skies and out-of-focus parts of a photo.

# Top 100

# Change images
# NONDESTRUCTIVELY

A RAW file is an incomplete photograph. You cannot simply display such an image file or even print from it without some sort of processing. You can always display a JPEG image in all sorts of programs on your computer, plus you could take a JPEG file right from the camera and get a print made.

A RAW file must be interpreted by software for it to become a photograph. When this interpretation is done, no changes are ever made to the original RAW file. All adjustments are actually instructions that the computer uses to interpret and process the RAW file. This is said to be *nondestructive processing* because no pixels from the original file are ever changed. This can be very freeing to the photographer because it means that he or she can try almost anything and never damage the original file.

When you open a RAW file from the Organizer or directly in the Editor, Camera Raw opens, which is Elements' RAW software.

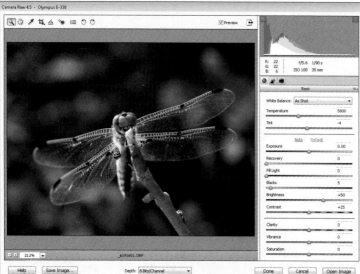

All adjustments are made as instructions as to how to convert the RAW file to a file that can be used in Photoshop Elements.

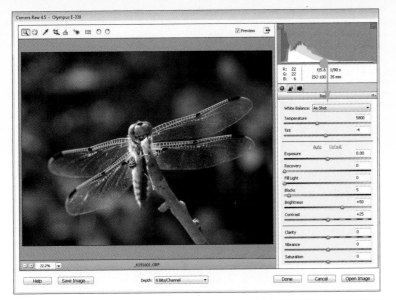

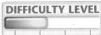
● The Camera Raw interface offers a lot of readily available adjustments that do not require you to go to a menu.

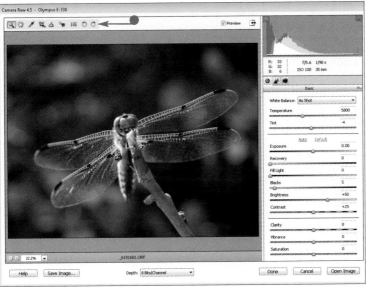

● The interface also includes a simple toolbox of frequently used tools for photographs.

TIPS

### Did You Know?

Whenever you work directly on a photograph in Photoshop Elements, you are working directly on pixels. Those pixels are then changed, which is called *destructive editing* because the original pixel data is "destroyed" as changes are applied. Camera Raw allows you to make nondestructive changes.

### Try This!

You can change the magnification of the displayed photo in Camera Raw by using the magnifier in the toolbox and clicking or dragging on the photograph. You can also click the magnification number at the lower left of the photograph to get a drop-down menu of specific magnification sizes.

### Did You Know?

JPEG is a processed RAW file. The camera takes the image data coming from the sensor and very quickly processes it. This is obviously a locked-down, processed RAW file. It is good that this file is processed optimally for the particular camera being used, and file size is much reduced, but it also means the flexibility of the original RAW file is lost.

# CROP YOUR PHOTOS
## to start your processing

The world does not always cooperate and give you the opportunity to make perfect pictures every time. Sometimes the world simply does not fit the frame defined by your camera frame. At other times, stuff creeps in along the edges of your picture that really does not belong with your subject.

You should remove these things from your photograph as soon as you start working on an image. This allows you to really focus on the important part of the picture and not be distracted by unimportant things. It also allows you to adjust the picture optimally for what needs to be adjusted and not be influenced by other parts of the original picture.

Cropping is what allows you to keep "the junk" out of your picture and refine it to the key elements of your subject and scene.

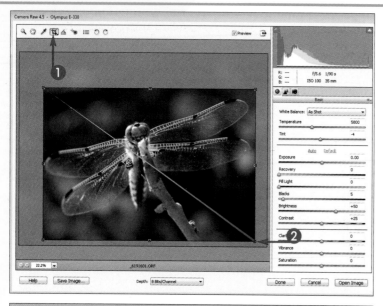

1 Click the Crop tool to select it.

2 Click and drag over the photo to start your crop.

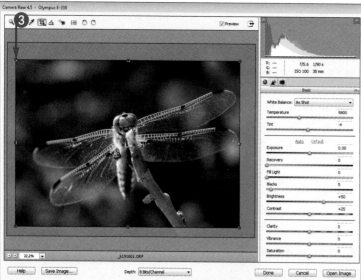

3 Drag the edges and corners of the crop box to make the cropped area larger or smaller.

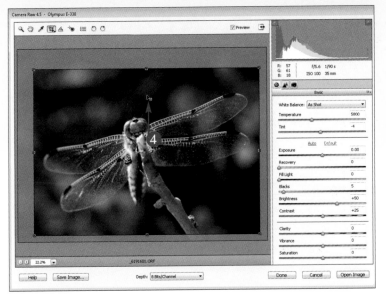

**4** Click and drag the photo itself to move it and fit it within the crop box.

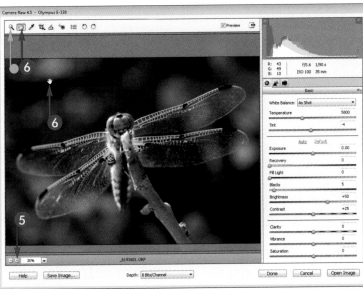

**5** Magnify the photo in the work area by using the –/+ signs at the lower left.

● You can also magnify the photo with the zoom magnifier tool.

**6** Use the Hand tool to reposition the photo in the work area because these changes can put parts of it out of view.

## TIPS

### Did You Know?
You can re-crop at any time. This is part of the whole idea of nondestructive processing of an image. Camera Raw remembers how you cropped a particular RAW file, and then lets you change that at any time.

### More Options!
You can rotate your crop box by simply moving your cursor outside of the box so that the cursor changes to a curved double-arrow cursor; then you click and drag to rotate. You can remove or clear your crop by right-clicking the photo to get a menu that includes Clear Crop.

### More Options!
You can crop to specific proportions within Camera Raw; however, they are not specific to inches. You can get the specific proportions by either right-clicking the photograph when using the Crop tool to get a context-sensitive menu, or by clicking and holding the Crop tool to get the same menu.

# ADJUST BLACKS AND WHITES
## to give a photo strength

Chapter 2 described the importance of adjusting blacks and whites in a photograph. This is a very important adjustment to make in Camera Raw because it sets the tonalities for everything else. You have even more flexibility and control when doing this in Camera Raw. You not only adjust the blacks and whites, but you can also adjust the brightness of the very dark areas and the very bright areas separately.

Blacks can be especially important in giving a photograph and its colors strength. Adjusting blacks is very subjective, but also very important. You will find that some photographs need minimal black, whereas others need quite large areas of black throughout the photograph. Photoshop Elements helps you out, in a way, by calling this adjustment Blacks. Whites are adjusted, on the other hand, by Exposure. Exposure should not actually be used for adjusting the overall brightness or darkness of the picture.

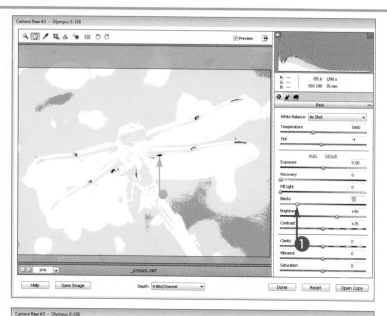

**❶** Press the Alt key and click and drag the Blacks slider.

The blacks threshold screen appears.

● Watch where the pure blacks and maxed-out channels appear.

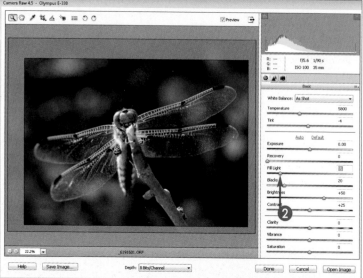

**❷** Adjust the Fill Light slider to give a boost to the darkest areas.

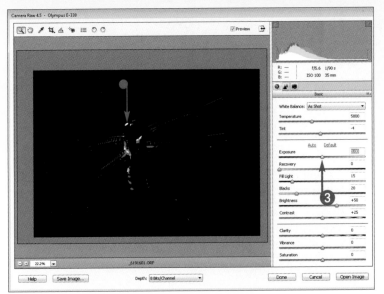

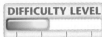

③ Press the Alt key and click and drag the Exposure (whites) slider.

The whites threshold screen appears.

● Watch where the pure whites and maxed-out channels appear.

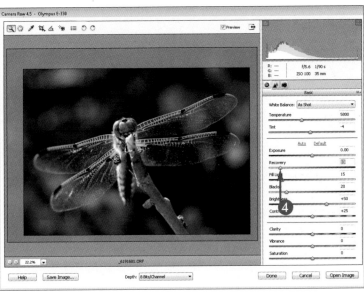

④ Adjust the Recovery slider when highlights look weak and washed out.

---

TIPS

### Did You Know?

Photographers often refer to the black areas of a photograph as the *blacks* but not because black comes in different brightnesses — it obviously does not. This use of the term *blacks* refers to all of the small areas of black scattered throughout the photograph.

### Did You Know?

Some people wonder why you need to adjust both the Blacks and Fill Light sliders. They seem to counteract each other. However, such an adjustment does give a different and better look to the dark areas of the picture than adjusting either one alone or not at all.

### Important!

Always adjust your blacks first, before Fill Light, before Exposure, and before Recovery. Setting your blacks right away allows you to better see your adjustments for tonality and color. If you adjust Fill Light first, you often find the picture starts looking very gray.

# ADJUST MIDTONES
## to make tonalities light or dark

In Chapter 2, you also learned about adjusting midtones in a photograph. Once again, this is a very important adjustment to make in Camera Raw. It makes the overall picture lighter or darker. This can help you make the picture look right so that it is neither dark and muddy nor bright and washed out. Adjusting your overall tonalities in Camera Raw allows you to get the optimum results from these tones as well.

Midtones are adjusted by two sliders in Camera Raw in Photoshop Elements: Brightness and Contrast. Often you will change only the Brightness slider, but just as often you will be adjusting both sliders. You would rarely adjust only the Contrast slider for most general types of photography, though it can be interesting for certain effects. Brightness and Contrast really do go well together for adjusting the midtones of your photograph.

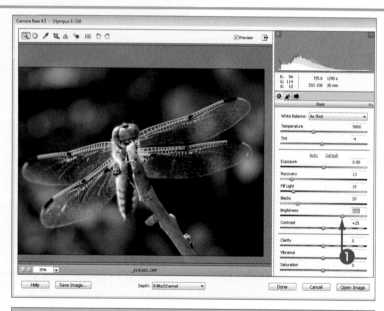

① Click and drag the Brightness slider to make the overall photo brighter or darker.

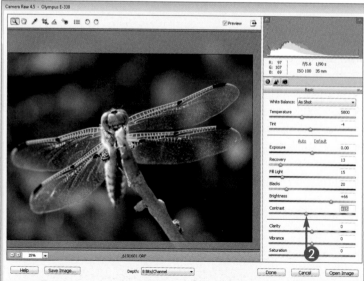

② Adjust the Contrast slider to affect the overall contrast of the photo.

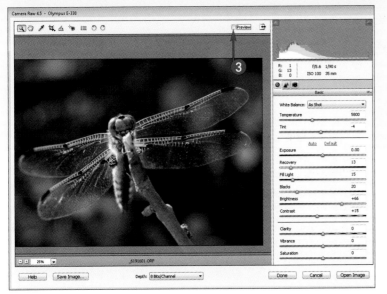

**3** Click the Preview on and off to compare before and after adjustments.

**DIFFICULTY LEVEL**

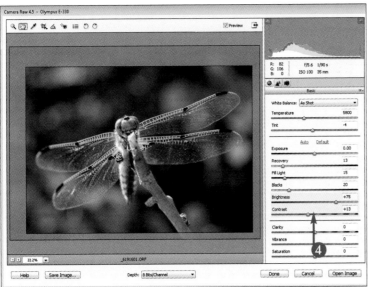

**4** Readjust Brightness and Contrast as needed to adapt to each of these control's changes.

### Important!

Adjust your blacks and whites first. Adjusting these tones truly does affect everything else in the photograph. Without a good black in the picture, especially, colors never look as good and images never print as well.

### Did You Know?

Color is strongly affected by the blacks, whites, and midtones in the picture. Color is not simply a part of your subject; it is actually very subjective and strongly affected by tones all around it. This is why adjusting your blacks, whites, and midtones before actually trying to control color is so important.

### Important!

RAW is no magic bullet that can correct a bad exposure. You do need to be sure that your bright areas, especially, are exposed properly in your image. RAW files do have a lot more flexibility in how you can adjust an image, but they cannot bring in detail or tones that the camera and sensor did not originally capture.

# CORRECT COLOR
## to clean up color casts

Color casts are slight tints of color that appear over the entire photograph. These can be both desirable and undesirable. If you are photographing at sunrise or sunset, you want a warm color cast for the photograph. But often, color casts are a problem. They keep you from clearly seeing the colors in a photograph and can put unwanted colors into neutral tones.

Unwanted color casts can be corrected very easily in Camera Raw. They are so easy to correct that you can quickly make a correction, then simply undo it or redo it as needed if you do not like it. Because everything in Camera Raw is nondestructive, this is never a problem. By repeatedly making corrections to color to clean up color casts in a photograph, you can actually learn a little bit about color casts and how to better see them.

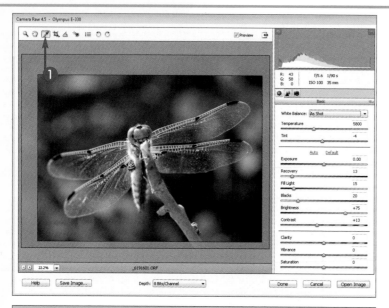

① Click the White Balance Tool (the eyedropper) in the toolbox.

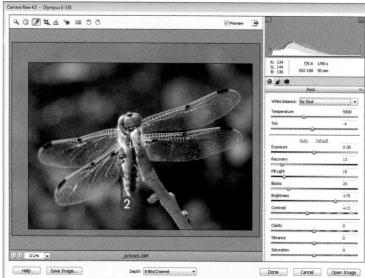

② Move the cursor into the photograph and click something that should be a neutral color.

66

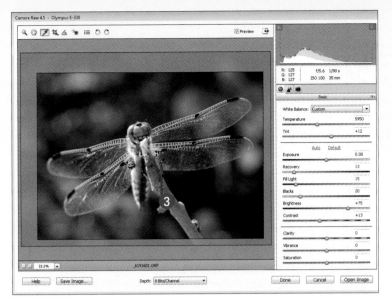

Camera Raw makes that neutral color neutral and removes a color cast.

③ Try clicking another location to see if you get a better color.

**DIFFICULTY LEVEL**

If the color looks good, you are done.

If the color looks really bad, press Ctrl+Z to undo the adjustment.

④ Change the Temperature and Tint sliders to further adjust the color.

---

## TIPS

### Try This!

You can use Camera Raw's white balance settings to affect your photograph. Click the White Balance arrow and you get a drop-down menu of white balance settings. Click any one to see what it looks like, and then use the up- and down-arrow keys to go through them all.

### Did You Know?

The white balance settings in Camera Raw look like the settings on a camera. You might think that they are the same settings and can be used in the same way. Although they are similar, these settings actually represent Adobe colors based on how Adobe engineers deal with colors for the settings.

### Important!

RAW is sort of a magic bullet when it comes to white balance. You can change your white balance settings as much as you want without any harm to the picture, plus you can adjust a picture that is way out of balance quite easily. Still it is best to actually select a white balance setting in your camera because this will make your colors more consistent.

---

# USE VIBRANCE AND CLARITY
## to intensify images

Vibrance and Clarity are two relatively new adjustments for Camera Raw in Photoshop Elements. Vibrance affects color. This control can either increase or decrease the intensity of a color. It is like Saturation, an older tool that is much more heavy-handed, but it does not oversaturate colors as easily. Vibrance also affects less-saturated colors more and has a strong effect on skies.

Clarity adjusts the contrast of midtones. This is a very visual effect that is hard to explain in words. A way to see this is to simply drag the slider all the way over to the right, look at the effects on the picture, and then drag the slider all the way to the left and see those effects as well. Then simply move the slider in the direction that seems best for your picture, but not at the extremes.

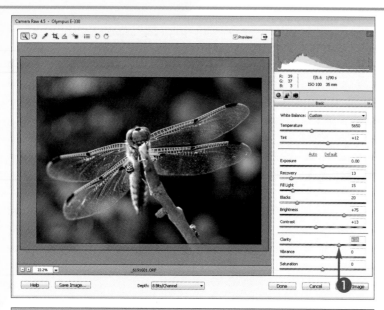

**①** For an image with interesting midtone detail, move the Clarity slider 30–40 points to the right.

**②** To give your photo a little boost in color, move the Vibrance slider 20–30 points to the right.

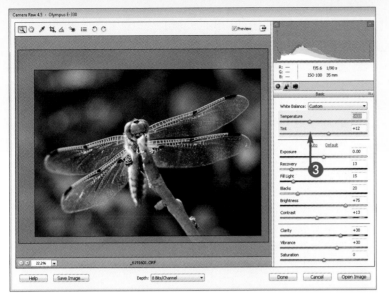

③ If the color looks good but seems to pick up a color cast, try adjusting the Temperature and Tint sliders.

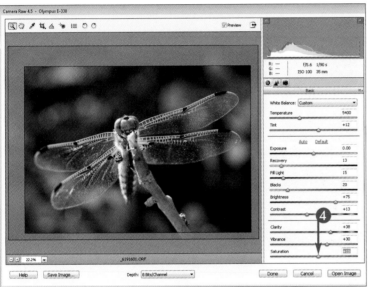

Be wary of using the Saturation slider because it is easy to overuse.

④ If you feel the photo still needs more lively colors, try using the Saturation slider up to about 12 points.

---

**TIPS**

### Try This!
Whenever you want to reset a slider in Camera Raw, simply double-click the slider itself. This immediately resets that slider to its default. This can be a good way of seeing exactly what your adjustment is doing to a picture. Just remember your setting before you double-click.

### Did You Know?
Some people confuse Clarity with sharpness. Clarity is not sharpness, but a way of affecting a very specific contrast within your picture — the contrast of midtones. This can make a picture look like it is being sharpened, but Clarity is not as refined an adjustment as sharpening.

### Attention!
Portraits and increased Clarity do not always go well together. Clarity intensifies pores, wrinkles, and defects in a person's skin, which is not always very flattering. In fact, portraits sometimes look better if Clarity is decreased so that skin texture is not as pronounced.

# SHARPEN PHOTOS
## with precision

Traditionally, the standard recommendation for sharpening your picture was always to sharpen at the very end of your processing. This is because some of the strong adjustments to a photograph can affect sharpening. However, the sharpening tools in Photoshop Elements Camera Raw offer new algorithms that really work quite well. In addition, you are doing most of your strong adjustments in Camera Raw, so it is appropriate to do sharpening here.

With experience, you might find that certain photographs do require much more adjustment in Photoshop Elements itself. When that happens, you may decide to do sharpening at the end of all your adjustments. Photoshop Elements does have good sharpening tools, so it is okay to do sharpening then instead of in Camera Raw. But if Camera Raw becomes an important part of your workflow, then you will do most of your sharpening in it.

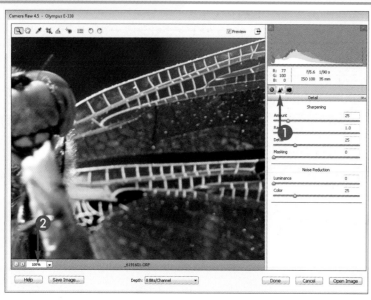

① Click the Detail tab in the adjustment panel on the right.

 This opens the Sharpening and Noise Reduction adjustments.

② Click 100% in the magnification menu at the lower left so that you can better see the sharpening effects.

③ Move the Amount slider to the right until the image starts to look sharp, but no more.

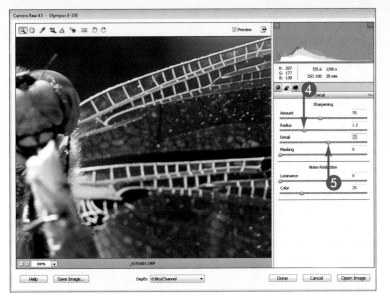

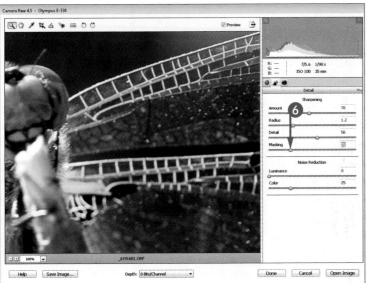

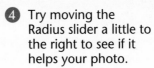
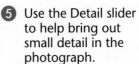

④ Try moving the Radius slider a little to the right to see if it helps your photo.

⑤ Use the Detail slider to help bring out small detail in the photograph.

⑥ Use the Masking slider to limit your sharpening to the strongest edges.

Masking can be very important when your subject is sharp and the background is out of focus.

**TIPS**

### Did You Know?
Amount controls the intensity of the sharpening. Radius affects how far sharpening is applied around pixel-sized detail. Detail modifies how strongly Radius interacts with Amount on details. Masking changes where sharpening is applied by blocking it from less-detailed areas.

### Try This!
Press and hold the Alt key as you adjust any of the Sharpening controls and the image changes to a black-and-white rendition of how that control is affecting the picture. Some photographers find this easier to actually see the sharpening effects because color can be distracting.

### Caution!
Avoid oversharpening your photos. Sharpening is not meant to make a blurry picture sharp. You need to get the best sharpness possible when you take the picture. Increasing the sharpening controls too much can make your picture look harsh and unappealing.

# CONTROL NOISE
## in your photo

Noise is inherently a part of digital photography. The latest cameras control noise extremely well, especially with proper exposure. However, every camera has its own noise characteristics for an image file. Cameras with smaller image sensors have more noise, higher ISOs increase noise, and underexposure of a scene also increases noise in the final picture. All of this makes noise show up more as you sharpen the photo.

This is why Camera Raw includes Noise Reduction in the Detail tab along with Sharpening. You can affect two types of noise — the sand-like pattern of luminance noise and the color pattern of color noise. This Noise Reduction works well for average amounts of noise in standard photographs. It really does not work that well for very strong or severe noise in an image. For that, you need special software designed specifically for noise reduction.

① Click 100–200% in the magnification menu at the lower left so that you can see noise more clearly.

② Press the spacebar to get the Hand tool and move the photo to find a dark, smooth area that shows noise.

③ Move the Luminance slider to the right until the noise starts to smooth out, but no more.

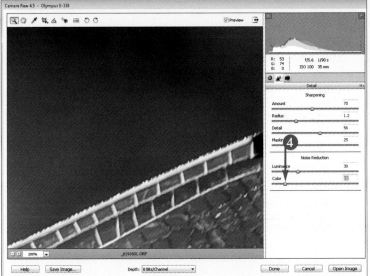

You can move the Color slider to the right if you see colored speckles that represent color noise.

④ Move the Color slider to the left from the default setting if, as in this example, there is no color noise present.

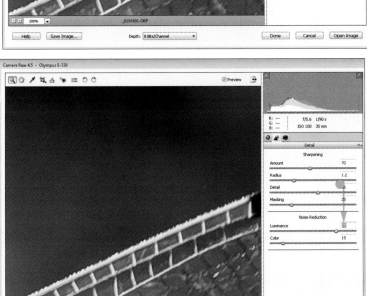

● Avoid high amounts of Luminance or Color noise reduction, as shown here, because this can adversely affect your photo.

---

## TIPS

### Did You Know?
Dark areas show noise more quickly than any other parts of a photograph when they are brightened. This is why you should avoid underexposing your pictures, forcing you to brighten dark areas, thereby increasing noise.

### Caution!
Noise is essentially tiny detail in your picture. Reducing noise can also reduce other tiny detail, so you need to be careful about how strongly you use the Noise Reduction sliders. The Color slider can also affect small but important color detail in your picture.

### Check It Out!
When noise starts to become very problematic in a photograph, you need to use other methods of noise reduction than what is available in Camera Raw. Dfine from Nik Software (www.niksoftware.com) or Noiseware from Imagenomic (www.imagenomic.com) are two programs that work quite well with Photoshop Elements. See task #85 for more about Dfine.

---

# Apply adjustments to
# MULTIPLE PHOTOS

Often, you will photograph a subject or scene in a variety of ways. Yet the exposure and the light is basically the same among all of these shots. It would take a lot of time to process each one of these pictures individually, but you do not have to. Camera Raw in Photoshop Elements allows you to apply multiple adjustments to photographs at the same time. This is a big timesaver. This is also a benefit for

photographers who shoot certain subjects in very standardized ways, such as portraits under a specific lighting setup. Portrait photographers, especially, often take a lot of pictures of a single subject or several subjects with little changes in exposure or lighting. Processing all of these pictures would really be a pain if you could not do something to adjust all of them very quickly.

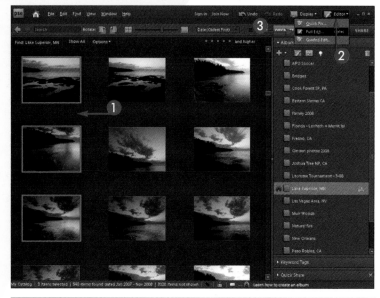

① Ctrl+click several similar RAW images in Organizer that need the same sorts of adjustments.

② Click Editor.

③ Click Full Edit to move the images to Camera Raw.

Camera Raw opens, now with a series of photos showing on the left.

④ Click the photo that can be adjusted most easily first.

That photo appears in the work area.

⑤ Click Select All to select the whole group of photos.

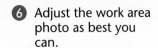

**6** Adjust the work area photo as best you can.

● Adjustments are automatically applied to the other photos, as well.

**# 32**

**DIFFICULTY LEVEL**

**7** Click any individual photo.

**8** Refine the adjustments on that photo as needed.

● Adjustments are only applied to this photo.

**TIPS**

### Try This!
You can use this technique when you want to change just one or two adjustments for your group of pictures and not have everything changed as you go. First make only those specific adjustments that you want to use across multiple pictures and do them for the selected group of pictures. Then go in and do the normal adjustments to individual pictures as needed.

### Check It Out!
As you make adjustments, you will find that there is an icon ( ) placed at the lower right-hand corner of your image that tells you adjustments have been made. This helps you keep track of which images have been adjusted if you are adjusting a group of photos one at a time.

### Warning!
As you adjust your photographs in Camera Raw, you will notice a small yellow triangle with an exclamation point in it appear in the upper right-hand corner of the images. This is a warning icon, but not something that you have to worry about. It simply says that your computer is working on processing these images for display.

# MOVE YOUR PICTURE
## to Photoshop Elements

Once you are done working on your image in Camera Raw, you need to move your picture to the Photoshop Elements Editor. Camera Raw is a separate program from Photoshop Elements, so you have to get your pictures out of that program and loaded into Editor.

Because everything done in Camera Raw is just instructions on how to process and convert the image from the RAW file to an actual picture file, that

conversion must occur for you to work on the image outside of Camera Raw. These instructions are also saved as a separate, companion file to your RAW file so that if you open that RAW file again in Camera Raw, all of your adjustments are still there. Because the RAW file cannot be changed, only converted, no adjustments are actually applied to any of the data in that file.

① Click the Depth pop-up menu.

② Choose 8 Bits/Channel.

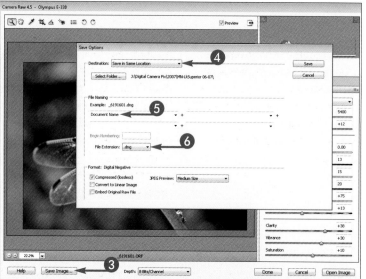

You can save your image converted to a specific format.

③ Click Save Image.

The Save Options dialog box appears.

④ Choose a destination.

⑤ Name your file.

⑥ Choose a file format.

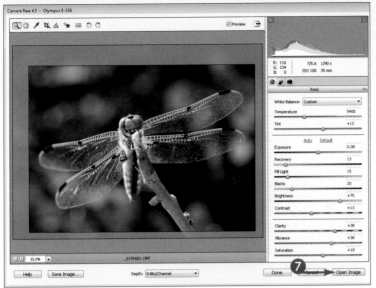

You can open your image directly into Photoshop Elements.

⑦ Click Open Image.

# 33

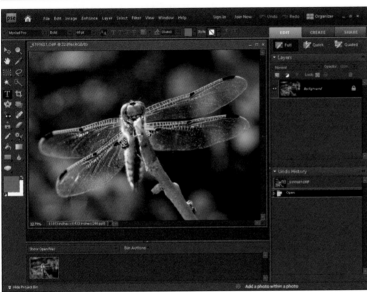

The photo opens into Photoshop Elements, converted from the RAW file based on the adjustments you made in Camera Raw.

---

 **TIPS**

### Did You Know?

Bit depth represents how much processing flexibility you have in an image file. You are processing in Camera Raw at the maximum capability of 16-bit. Unless you are planning to do a lot of processing in Photoshop Elements, you can easily use the smaller 8-bit file there.

### More Options!

When using Save As, you can choose a number of possibilities, including PSD for processing later in Photoshop Elements, JPEG for Web use or small archival files, TIFF for use with publications, and DNG, Adobe's general purpose RAW file.

### Try This!

If you find you consistently adjust your images in a certain way, you can reset Camera Raw defaults so that these adjustments are always done to an image as soon as it opens. Make those adjustments to a file and then click the icon with three lines (⚏). Choose Save New Camera Raw Defaults from the menu that appears.

---

# Choose Local Control Features

The real world is often quite different than the photograph that your camera captures. This is not your or the camera's fault; it is simply a reflection of the fact that the camera sees the world differently than people do. One very common problem is that the camera makes certain things brighter or darker in proportion to other objects in the scene compared to the way that you actually see them. Another problem is that color relationships are often recorded differently compared to the way people see them.

A way to correct these problems is to isolate them in a photograph so that they can be adjusted separately from the rest of the image. This is called *local control* as compared to overall or global control over the whole image. This type of work with an image was very common when photographers spent time in the traditional darkroom. It used to be hard to do with color photography, but the computer changed that. With Photoshop Elements, you have the ability to select and isolate very specific parts of the picture and then make corrections just to that isolated area so that no other parts of the picture are affected. That is a very important control for a photographer.

# Top 100

# Create and use
# A SELECTION

Selections are a key way of isolating a part of the picture for adjustment separate from the rest. A selection is a little bit like building a fence. If you build a fence in the middle of a field and put all the cows in there, they eat the grass there and nowhere else. If you create a selection in the middle of the picture, any adjustments that you make are done inside that selection and nowhere else.

Photoshop Elements offers a number of ways to create selections, and you will learn them in this chapter. The reason for the choice of selections is to make selections easier, more effective, and more precise for specific needs of individual pictures. In this task, you will learn what a selection can do, how it works, and how it combines with adjustments to control where an adjustment occurs.

**①** Open a photo in the Editor.

**②** Select the Rectangular Selection tool in the toolbox.

**③** Click and drag a rectangular selection inside your picture.

④ Click Enhance, Adjust Lighting, and then Levels to open the Levels dialog box.

⑤ Make an extreme adjustment with Levels so that you can see the effect.

⑥ Click Cancel.

# 34

DIFFICULTY LEVEL

⑦ Click Enhance, Adjust Color, and then Adjust Hue/Saturation to open the Hue/Saturation dialog box.

⑧ Click the Colorize check box (■ changes to ☑).

⑨ Make an extreme adjustment with Saturation so that you can see the effect.

⑩ Click Cancel.

TIPS

### Remember This!

Always remember to do a Save As for any JPEG files that you open into Photoshop Elements. You can save these files as either a PSD or a TIFF file for further work in the program. This protects your original file. Doing this with a RAW file is also helpful, but you do not have to worry about protecting the original file in that case.

### Change It!

Once you have a selection, you can easily get rid of it and start a new selection at any time. You can use the keyboard by pressing Ctrl+D to deselect your selection. You can also click your cursor outside of a selection to deselect as well, as long as you are still using a selection tool.

### Did You Know?

Colorize is an interesting part of Hue/Saturation because it does not simply change colors in a picture — it adds colors to a picture. When you click that check box, the adjustment adds whatever color is chosen in the Hue area to the photograph. You can then adjust the intensity of this color by using the Saturation slider.

# USE MARQUEE TOOLS
## for specific shapes

The rectangular and elliptical selection tools in the toolbox are called the marquee selection tools. They both sit in the same place at the upper-left side of the toolbox. By default, the Rectangular Marquee tool is visible. The Elliptical Marquee tool is "underneath" the rectangle. You can get at the elliptical tool by clicking and holding on the rectangle until a small menu appears that shows both tools. You then select the one you want.

The rectangular and elliptical tools give you exactly what you expect, rectangle and ellipse shapes. They are great to experiment with when you are learning selections because they are so obvious. Their shapes are so specific, however, that most photographers use them infrequently because most photographs do not commonly have these very specific shapes. Still, when you do need them, they give you very specific and precise shapes in a hurry.

### USE THE RECTANGULAR MARQUEE TOOL

1 Select the Rectangular Marquee tool in the toolbox.

2 Click and drag a selection around an area that works with the shape.

3 Choose an adjustment appropriate for the selected area inside your photograph.

4 Make the adjustment.

   In this example, the midtones are adjusted slightly darker.

5 Click OK.

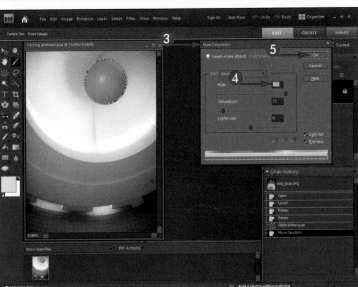

1 Select the Elliptical Marquee tool in the toolbox.

2 Click and drag a selection around an area that works with the shape.

The elliptical tool takes some practice getting used to.

Experiment with it to see how it might work for you.

DIFFICULTY LEVEL

3 Open an adjustment appropriate for the selected area inside your photograph.

4 Make the adjustment.

5 Click OK.

## TIPS

### More Options!

The Marquee tool also does the square and circle selections. To get a square, choose the Rectangular Marquee tool and press and hold the Shift key as you make the selection. To create a circular selection, choose the Elliptical Marquee tool and press and hold the Shift key again as you make the selection.

### Try This!

Once you have created a selection, you can move it to a better place in your photograph as needed. Simply click inside the selection area while pressing and holding the mouse button. You must keep the mouse button held down while you do this. Then drag the selection to a new area. You can also move your selection with the arrow keys.

### More Options!

If you look closely, you notice that a lot of the tools in the toolbox have a little black triangle to the bottom right of the icon. This indicates that more tools are available than what is showing. Clicking and holding on the icon reveals a stack of tools.

# USE LASSO TOOLS
## to follow picture elements

The rectangular and elliptical selection tools are pretty restrictive as to what they can do in a photograph. Most photographs do not have such specific shapes. Photoshop Elements gives you additional freehand tools for selecting in any shape: the Lasso, the Polygonal Lasso, and the Magnetic Lasso tools.

The Polygonal Lasso is probably the easiest to use for most photographers. You simply click the place to start and then move your cursor along a selection,

clicking as you go to anchor the selection. You complete the selection by clicking the beginning point or double-clicking. The Magnetic Lasso is an automated Lasso that finds edges for you. If you have a strong edge where your selection needs to be, you start this tool near that edge and it finds the edge for you. The Lasso works totally freehand, going wherever your cursor goes, but it can be hard to control without a lot of practice.

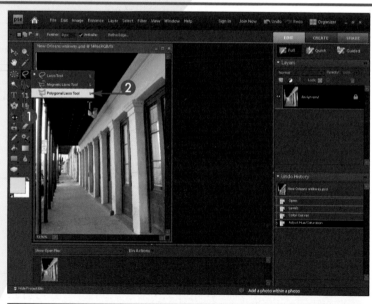

**1** Click and hold on the lasso tool.

**2** Select the Polygonal Lasso tool.

**3** Click at one edge where you want to make a selection.

**4** Move the cursor along the edge, clicking regularly to anchor the selection edge.

● The selection edge follows your cursor.

⑤ Click and move your cursor all around the area that you want to select.

⑥ Finish the selection by clicking where you started.

The cursor adds a small o at its lower right when it is over the starting point.

⑦ Choose an adjustment appropriate for the selected area inside your photograph.

⑧ Make the adjustment.

In this example, the ceiling has been lightened.

⑨ Click OK.

The adjustment is now made only inside the selected area.

---

 **TIPS**

## Important!

Selections take practice. When you first start using selections, you may find it frustrating to make your selections go exactly where you want them. With practice, you get much better. You can also find ideas in the rest of this chapter that make creating selections easier.

## Try This!

The Magnetic Lasso is very useful when you have a picture in which your subject, for example, contrasts strongly against a simple background. This selection tool looks for contrasting edges and finds them for you. This makes selection easy as long as you have those edges.

## More Options!

Because the Polygonal Lasso goes in a straight line from click to click, you might think that it is not useful for curves. In fact, this tool is actually good for curves because it is so controllable. What you have to do is move your cursor in short distances as you click around a curve.

# USE AUTOMATED TOOLS
## for easy selections

Photoshop Elements offers a diversity of selection tools so that you have options for matching a tool with the selection challenge in a photograph. Adobe has even added some automated tools that help you find edges and create selections quickly for certain types of pictures. One of them, the Magnetic Lasso, was described in the previous task.

Three more very useful automated selection tools are the Magic Wand, the Selection Brush, and the Quick

Selection tool. The Magic Wand is used for areas that have a consistent tone or color. Click that area and the Magic Wand finds all pixels similar to the color and tone where you clicked. The Selection Brush allows you to literally paint a selection in the picture by brushing your cursor over an area. The Quick Selection Tool is sort of in between. You use it to brush through an area; it finds additional pixels that match that area in tone and color.

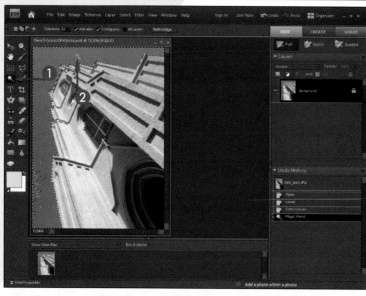

① Click the Magic Wand in the toolbox.

② Click in an even toned and colored area to begin the selection.

A selection is created based on the color and tone where you click.

③ Change the Tolerance for the tool if the selection goes too far or too little.

④ Click the tool twice: once to remove the old selection, again to create a new selection.

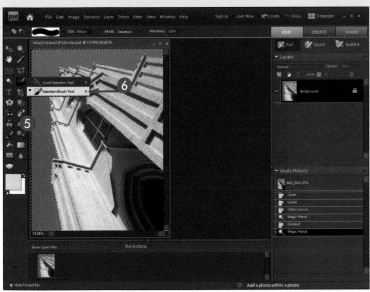

## 37

**5** Click and hold on the tool to the right of the Magic Wand.

**6** Choose the Selection Brush.

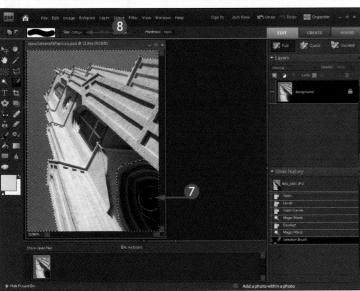

**7** Paint over an area you want to select using the Selection Brush.

**8** Change the Size if the brush is too big or small for the area.

## TIPS

### More Options!

The Contiguous check box for the Magic Wand is a very useful option. When it is checked, the selection captures only contiguous or connected areas. When it is unchecked, the selection looks for any places in your photograph that have the same colors and tone, connected or not.

### More Options!

The Tolerance setting for the Magic Wand is an important option. This tells the tool how to look at tones and colors within the picture to make the selection. Set it lower to restrict your selection and higher to make it find more parts of the picture.

### Save It!

Once you have a good selection, you may want to keep it so that you can go back to the selection later. You can save that selection. Go up to the Select menu and then click Save Selection. Give the selection a name, keep New Selection checked, and click OK.

# EXPAND OR CONTRACT
## your selection

After you create a selection, you often find that it is not quite right. That is normal. Making a perfect selection in one try can be really difficult. Luckily, Photoshop Elements has features that allow you to refine a selection and make it do what you want it to do. You can easily add to a selection or subtract from a selection as needed.

This is very important because it makes selecting easier. You do not have to worry about making a selection perfect right from the start. In fact, making your first selection very quickly and then refining that selection to the final area is often easier and faster than trying to do it entirely right as you go. No matter what you do, you will often find little jags, corners, and other odd shapes are easier to deal with after you have done your first selection work.

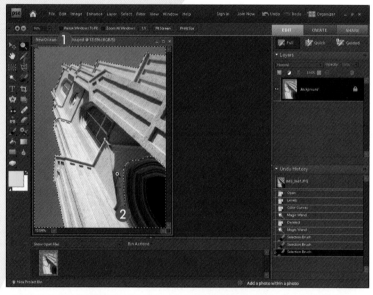

① Click the Zoom tool in the toolbox.

**Note:** *It usually helps to magnify the selected area so you can better see the edges.*

② Click and drag the magnifier around the area to magnify it.

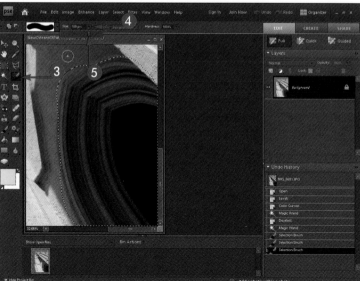

③ Select the Selection Brush.

④ Click the arrow at the right of the brush size box.

A size slider appears.

⑤ Change the brush to a small size appropriate to the areas you need to refine.

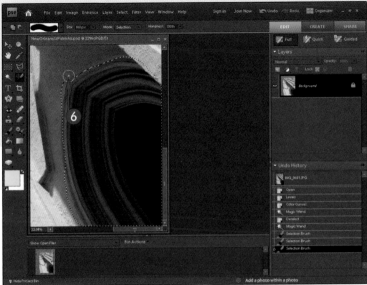

**6** Press the Alt key and then click and drag the Brush tool to remove part of a selection.

Remove all excess selection areas.

## 38

**DIFFICULTY LEVEL**

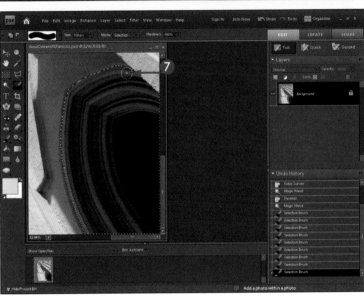

**7** Use a brush sized appropriately to add specific areas to a selection.

Refine your selection by going back and forth between the default add function and the Alt key subtract function of the brush.

---

**TIPS**

### Try This!
The Lasso tool is ideal for adding and subtracting from a selection. It can be hard to use when trying to make a large selection, but for little adjustments, it works well. Press and hold the Alt key to remove part of a selection and hold down the Shift key to add to a selection when using the Lasso tool.

### More Options!
You might have noticed that your cursor changed when it went over the word Size in the options bar. Your cursor becomes activated and you can simply click and drag left and right to make the brush size smaller or larger, respectively. Many numerical options in Photoshop Elements work this way.

### Try This!
You can make your brush size larger or smaller very quickly by using the keyboard. To the right of the letter P are the bracket keys, [ and ]. Press the [ and the brush gets smaller. Press the ] and the brush gets larger. You will find this is very handy for sizing your brush to the perfect size.

# SELECT WHAT IS EASY
## and invert

Photographs can be challenging at times. You want to make an adjustment to a very specific part of the picture, but selecting around that area is difficult.

One way to deal with this is to look at your picture carefully before you start making a selection. You may discover selecting something beside your subject or other area that you really want to select is easier. That would not help you if that were all you could do, because you do not want to select that area.

However, Photoshop Elements enables you to make a selection and then invert it or flip it over so that what was selected is now unselected and what was unselected is now selected. Often when you look at a picture you can find easier ways of making a selection than simply going around what really needs to be selected in the end.

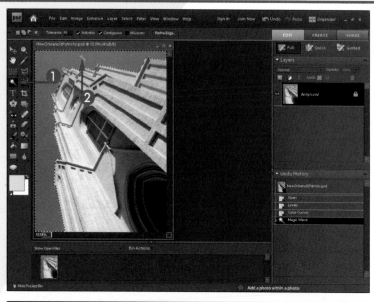

*Note: Skies are often very easy to select with the Magic Wand and can be used to start a selection around a complex shape.*

① Click the Magic Wand in the toolbox.

② Click the sky to begin the selection.

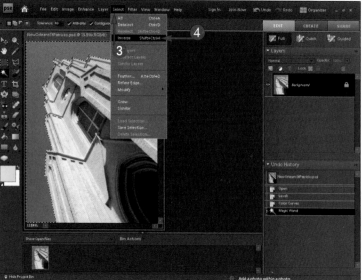

③ Click Select.

④ Choose Inverse.

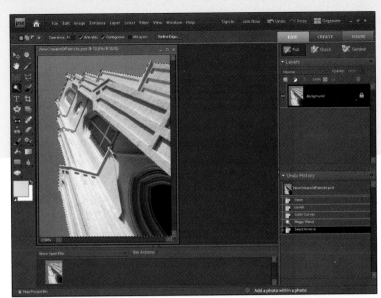

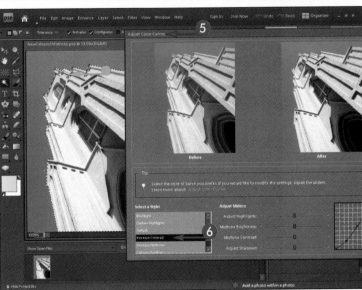

⑤ Open an adjustment dialog box.

⑥ Make an adjustment.

● The adjustment applies to the area you originally wanted to work on, but not to the sky.

## TIPS

### More Options!

Remember that you do not have to do a complete selection in one try. You can use this technique to do the best you can, such as selecting the sky and inverting the selection. Then you can add to that selection or subtract from it using other selection tools. Simply press and hold the Shift key while selecting to add or the Alt key to subtract.

### Try It!

Sometimes the outline around your selection can be distracting. Ctrl+H temporarily hides the selection outline, yet the selection is still there. Press Ctrl+H again and the selection outline reappears. Do not forget that you used this command or you will get frustrated that controls are not working right because of a "hidden" selection.

### Put It Together!

Use whatever selection tools make it easiest to get your selection started. Then use the Inverse command as well as adding to and subtracting from a selection to refine your selection as needed. Using multiple tools like this helps a lot in getting better selections.

# BLEND EDGES
## by feathering

Selections create a very hard edge between the selected and unselected areas, a hard edge that is really not normal in a photograph. Magnify any photograph, and you rarely see a razor-sharp edge anywhere. This is because of the way light works as well as how things go in and out of focus in an image. Using an unmodified selection this way can look very unnatural in the picture.

Elements does give you the opportunity to make this edge blend in. This is called *feathering*. Feathering has to be adjusted for every selection, because how much of a blend is needed depends entirely on the subject in the photograph. This is why it is best to do the feathering after you have made a selection, because if you do not like the feathering you simply undo it and try another amount. The selection remains unchanged.

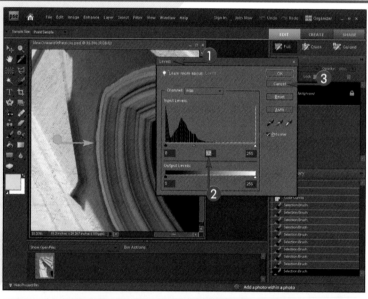

**1** Open an adjustment control to affect something in a selection.

**2** Make a strong adjustment so that the difference really shows up between selected and unselected areas.

● Note the hard edge between adjusted and unadjusted areas.

Ctrl+H hides the selection outline to make the edge easier to see.

**3** Click Cancel.

**4** Click Select.

**5** Choose Feather.

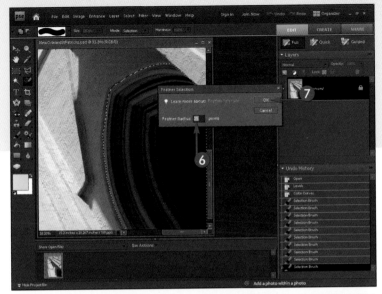

The Feather Selection dialog box opens.

**⑥** Type a moderate number for Feather Radius such as 25.

*Note: The amount of Radius is relative and will be "large," "moderate," or "small" based on the size of the selection.*

**⑦** Click OK.

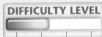

**DIFFICULTY LEVEL**

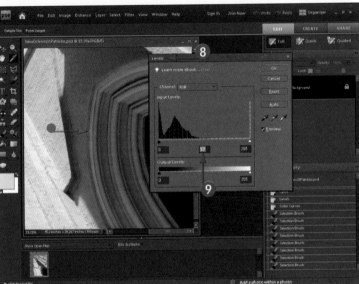

**⑧** Open an adjustment dialog box.

**⑨** Make a strong adjustment now.

● Note how the adjustment now blends nicely in the photo.

---

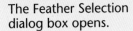

## TIPS

### More Options!

You can get a feathered edge to your selection when using the Selection Brush by choosing a soft-edge brush. After selecting the Selection Brush, right-click in the photograph to get choices of brush sizes. You can see the difference between a soft- and hard-edge brush there by the softness or hardness of the little circles.

### Did You Know!

When you choose an adjustment control after making a selection, the dialog box that opens shows you what is happening only inside the selection. For example, Levels shows something distinctly different for the selection than if you use Levels for the entire picture. The control is affecting only that selected area.

### Change It!

Feathering values affect how far a selection blends between the selected and unselected areas. If the photograph has fairly sharp edges as in the example, you typically use a low number, such as 5–10. If there is no sharp edge or you want the blend to cross a wider part of the picture, use a high number, such as 60–100.

# Use selections for
# TRADITIONAL EDGE DARKENING

Photographers working in the traditional darkroom typically would add a little bit of darkness along the edges of their pictures. This was called *burning in* the edges because of the way light was used to darken these edges. Ansel Adams considered this a critical part of working on an image in the darkroom. He felt that the viewer's eye had a tendency to drift off of a photograph because of the surroundings. Darkening the edge would help keep the viewer's eye in the photograph.

You can do this by using a selection. How much you darken an edge is very subjective and depends on your photograph. You do not want to make the effect too obvious, and you want to keep a good blend across the edge between the darkening and the rest of the photograph. Once you try this, you will discover that it gives your picture a livelier look.

① Choose the Lasso tool from the toolbox.

② Draw a rough outline all around the photograph, in from the edges but away from your main subject.

③ Open the Feather Selection control from the Select menu.

④ Type a large number for Feather Radius, such as 140–200.

⑤ Click OK.

The selection outline smoothes its shape, though you cannot see the actual feathering yet.

**6** Click Select.

**7** Select Inverse.

## 41

DIFFICULTY LEVEL

The selection now is along the outside edges of the image.

**8** Click Enhance, Adjust Lighting, and then Brightness/Contrast to open the Brightness/Contrast dialog box.

**9** Click and drag the Brightness slider to the left to darken the outside edges of the photograph.

Ctrl+H hides the selection outline to make the edge easier to see.

**10** Click the Preview check box on and off to see how the effect works.

## TIPS

### Attention!
Brightness/Contrast seems like it would be a good all-around adjustment for photographers. It is not. Its use should be restricted to special purposes such as darkening the outside edges of a photograph. It is a rather blunt-edged instrument for most adjustments in a photograph.

### Test It!
Experiment with feathering. Feathering is not some absolute thing for which you can pick an arbitrary number and be done with it. The same feathering numbers can look perfect on one photograph and awful on another. It is okay to try a number, do the adjustment, undo the effect if you dislike it, and try again.

### Did You Know?
Ansel Adams was a master landscape photographer who spent a lot of time in a traditional darkroom. He felt that the original exposure was only an approximation of what he really saw at the scene. He used his time in the darkroom to bring out the best in his images so that the scene was interpreted closer to the way he actually saw it.

# USE THE SMART BRUSH
## for specific area fixes

Beginning with Photoshop Elements 7, Adobe has introduced a special brush that allows you to brush on local adjustments in a photograph. The Smart Brush combines the Selection Brush with a whole range of preset adjustments that you choose and then use on your photograph. These adjustments very specifically define how such things as color, contrast, and special effects are applied to your photograph in restricted areas. They are easy to use, and so they are well

worth experimenting with to see what all the presets can do for your photographs. Some photographers find all of the presets very useful, whereas others use only a limited group.

Although you do not have to know anything about layers or layer masks in order to use the Smart Brush, this tool does use layers and layer masks for its effects. You will see a new layer appear in the Layers palette when you use the brush.

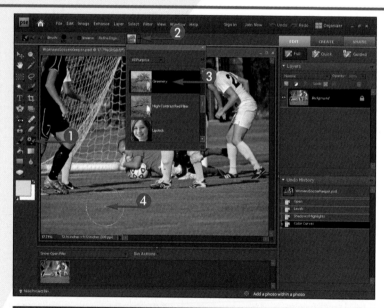

① Choose the Smart Brush from the toolbox.

② Click the Preset selector.

③ Choose the preset appropriate to your photo's needs.

   In this example, the Greenery adjustment was chosen to brighten the field.

④ Change the size of your brush with the [ and ] keys until it is sized correctly for the space.

⑤ Brush the preset change onto the photo over the area that needs the adjustment.

⑥ Add or subtract from the changed area with the plus and minus brushes.

Examine the change; if it is good, continue working on the photo.

⑦ Click the first Smart Brush icon to start a new Smart Brush adjustment using the same adjustments

This allows you to do the same adjustment, but at different locations and amounts.

⑧ Click the red Smart Brush icon to refine the adjustment.

*Note: The Smart Brush working icons change color as you add Smart Brush adjustments.*

A dialog box opens that automatically gives you the correct adjustment controls.

⑨ Change the adjustment to refine the work that the Smart Brush did.

This adjustment is up to you and will vary depending on the type of brush you chose.

In this image, the saturation of the grass was changed.

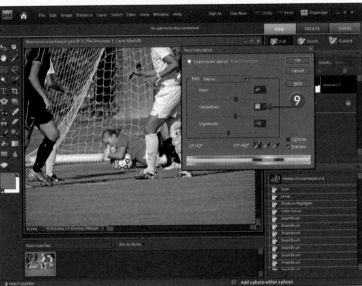

**# 42**

**DIFFICULTY LEVEL**

---

## TIPS

### Did You Know?

The Smart Brush is a very handy tool because you can reopen its adjustment and readjust the controls as much as you want. No harm will come to your picture when doing this, which makes it a great tool to experiment with. Just click the appropriate Smart Brush working icon for each adjustment.

### Did You Know?

Layers are a way of working with a photograph to keep adjustments separate from one another. They also allow you to make temporary adjustments to a picture that can be adjusted again and again without harming the picture. You will learn more about layers in the next chapter.

### Test It!

To totally remove a Smart Brush adjustment, you need to remove the layer on which the adjustment was made. That is easy to do. Simply go to the Layers palette, click the layer named for the adjustment you want to remove, and then drag it to the trash can icon above the layers. This is explained in more detail in the next chapter.

# Create Adjustment Layers for Nondestructive Changes

Photoshop Elements is pixel-editing software, designed to work with the pixels of a digital image. This is what you have been doing in the book so far except for your work with the Smart Brush in task #42. One problem with working directly on the pixels of an image is that every time they are changed, there is the potential for the loss of image quality as the pixel data changes. The pixels cannot gain more information, but they can lose it.

You can work on your image without changing any pixels through the use of adjustment layers and layer masks. A lot of photographers who have not used layers panic and do not want

anything to do with them. That is a big mistake. Adjustment layers give you a huge range of flexibility and power that you simply do not get when working directly on the pixels of an image.

Adjustment layers are actually a lot like filters on the camera. If you put a filter on your lens, you know that the scene does not change, but it does look different coming through the lens and onto your sensor. An adjustment layer is doing something very similar, changing the look of the pixels of a photograph yet not actually changing any pixel of that underlying picture.

# Top 100

# Understand
# HOW LAYERS WORK

If you turn away from Photoshop Elements for a minute, you will discover that you already know quite a bit about layers. Your keyboard on your desk is a layer. A book is made up of many layers of pages. Why is it that you cannot see the filling of a pie that has a big top crust? Because that top crust is a layer.

This is important to keep in mind because layers in Photoshop Elements really act the same way. They are simply a stack of digital things, from adjustment

layers to actual photographs, that act like any other layer stack. The stack has a top and a bottom, the top covers up everything underneath it, and you examine a stack from top to bottom. In addition, if you put a piece of green cellophane over a real-world stack, everything looks green, even though nothing has actually changed. The same thing happens with Photoshop Elements.

- This photo looks perfectly normal, except that what you are seeing is the result of layers, which are shown in the Layers palette.

- The original photo is at the bottom, but you are not seeing that.

- A solid sky layer blocks any view of the original photo, just as if you painted blue on a piece of plastic over a photo.

  Just like the paint on plastic, the original photo is still there, unharmed.

- The rocks have been copied to a new layer.

- The Joshua tree has also been copied to a new layer.

- Even though these layers have separate picture elements, they combine visually to look exactly like the original photo.

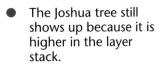

- The sky has been moved up in the layer stack, now blocking the view of the rocks.

- The rocks are still there, but because layers affect what is underneath them, the sky keeps the rocks hidden.

- The Joshua tree still shows up because it is higher in the layer stack.

  Layers always work so that higher layers affect layers underneath them.

  Because layers separate parts of a photo, you can easily change one part without affecting another.

- Now the photo just looks like rocks and sky.

- The original photo is still there, untouched.

- The rocks have been moved to the top of the layer stack.

- The Joshua tree has been moved to below the solid sky, so the sky hides the tree.

## 43

**DIFFICULTY LEVEL**

**TIPS**

### Did You Know?

If for any reason you discover that your palettes are not appearing, go to the Window menu. This menu has a whole list of items to display in the Photoshop Elements interface. You can turn any of them on or off by clicking the name of the palette.

### Try This!

Layers are easily moved up and down in the Layers palette. Simply click a layer and drag it to a new position. Photoshop Elements automatically opens a space for it and shifts the other layers to make room for it.

### Did You Know?

The biggest benefit of layers for the average photographer is the ability to isolate parts of a photo. This allows you to work separately on those parts, and having layers gives more options on how you can blend separate elements in different layers.

# Understand
# HOW ADJUSTMENT LAYERS WORK

Adjustment layers include many of the adjustment controls that you have seen in the book so far. An adjustment layer even shows the same controls, such as the Levels adjustment — the dialog box is identical for adjusting the photograph directly or with an adjustment layer.

Yet an adjustment layer is considerably different from adjusting on the photograph. These special layers are basically just instructions. As you make an adjustment,

the underlying picture appears to change, yet it really does not. What changes is the view through the adjustment layer. This is a very real adjustment, but it does not change pixels. That means you can adjust and readjust the controls in an adjustment layer as much as you want because the underlying picture never changes. This also means that the adjustments are nondestructive because pixels are not damaged in any way. In this task you will try an adjustment layer to see how these layers work.

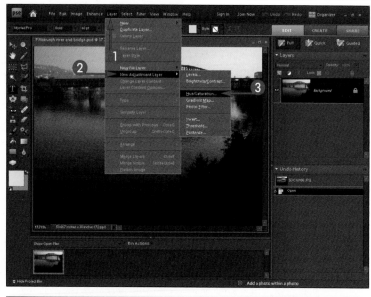

USE THE MENU TO ADD AN ADJUSTMENT LAYER

① Click Layer.

② Select New Adjustment Layer.

③ Choose Hue/Saturation.

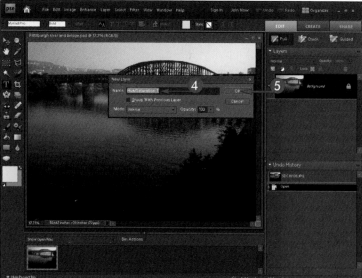

A New Layer dialog box opens.

④ You can change the layer's name to Color by typing it into the Name box or leave it at Hue/Saturation 1.

Leave the rest of the options alone and go with the defaults.

⑤ Click OK.

A Hue/Saturation adjustment layer is then created and the Hue/Saturation dialog box appears.

## USE THE ICON TO ADD AN ADJUSTMENT LAYER

① Click the Adjustment Layer icon at the top of the Layers palette.

② Choose Hue/Saturation.

**DIFFICULTY LEVEL**

● The Hue/Saturation dialog box opens; it looks identical to the dialog box that you open from the Adjust Lighting option under the Enhance menu.

● The difference is that an adjustment layer appears automatically over the original picture, now the background layer.

---

**TIPS**

### Did You Know?

Opening an adjustment layer with the icon on the Layers palette is quick and easy. Opening an adjustment layer with the Layer menu allows you to name the layer immediately and change its blending mode, opacity, and how it is grouped with other layers.

### Try This!

Naming your layers can be very useful to help you keep track of what they are doing to your picture. You can name or rename a layer at any time by simply double-clicking the name in the layer and typing a new name.

### Did You Know?

The extra choices that show up when you click the Adjustment Layer icon in the Layers palette are called *fill layers*. These unique layers let you add a color, gradient, or pattern to a layer stack. They are also easily adjustable and do not change the underlying photograph.

---

# HOW ADJUSTMENT LAYERS WORK

Once you start working with adjustment layers, you will probably use them most of the time when beginning your adjustments on the photograph. There will be times when you want to adjust the picture directly, such as when working very quickly on a picture that you do not need to change. Then you will not use an adjustment layer. But the advantages of using an adjustment layer are so great that you will find it really worth learning to use them and putting them into your normal workflow.

Adjustment layers mean that you can adjust and readjust a picture always at maximum quality. This is quite simple to do. You double-click the adjustment layer icon with the gears in it. The adjustment dialog box immediately reopens and you can make any changes you want. This allows you to tweak an image as you adjust it and discover that earlier adjustments were not done the way you want.

### APPLY AN ADJUSTMENT LAYER

① Repeat the steps from the previous page to open the Hue/Saturation dialog box.

② Click Colorize (■ changes to ☑).

③ Change the Hue and Saturation sliders so the picture looks like it was shot with a strongly colored filter.

④ Click OK.

⑤ Click the eye icon at the left of the adjustment layer in the Layers palette.

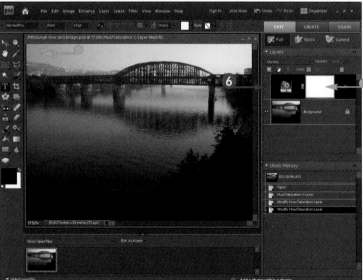

● The color goes away, yet the adjustment layer is still in the Layers palette.

⑥ Click the eye icon again.

The color comes back.

Clicking the eye icon simply turns the visibility of a layer on and off.

⑦ Double-click the icon in the adjustment layer and the adjustment reopens.

⑧ Change the Hue and Saturation sliders to change the color again.

Note the underlying picture is not affected, yet the photograph has changed.

**TIPS**

### Important!
When the adjustment dialog box of an adjustment layer is open, nothing else in the Photoshop Elements interface is accessible. For example, you cannot click the eye icon and make the layer visibility change if the Hue/Saturation adjustment dialog box is open.

### Try This!
Using Hue/Saturation to colorize an image can be an interesting way to create a one-color or monochrome photograph. You can change the hue to give the color a bluish cast, a sepia tone, and more. This is a simple way of changing the picture without actually getting rid of the original color picture.

### Important!
When you have layers and save your photograph with a PSD or Photoshop file format, all of those layers are saved with the file. You can close that image and open it days later — all of the layers will still be there. In fact, you can double-click an adjustment layer and go back to exactly what you used before or change it.

# WORK BLACKS AND WHITES
## with a Levels adjustment layer

The workflow that you followed in the first part of this book for adjusting an image is still important: set blacks and whites, adjust midtones, correct color, and so on. Now, however, instead of making these adjustments directly to the picture, you will be making the adjustments with adjustment layers.

Start by adjusting blacks and whites with Levels. Blacks and whites are so critical to how the rest of the picture looks, from its contrast to its colors, that this

is a very good place to start your work on an image. Blacks are very subjective. You adjust them differently depending on the subject, your interpretation of that scene, and your experience with working on pictures. Whites are very sensitive and usually have a more limited range of proper adjustment. It is a good idea to name this Levels layer **Blacks-Whites** so you know what it is doing as you add layers later.

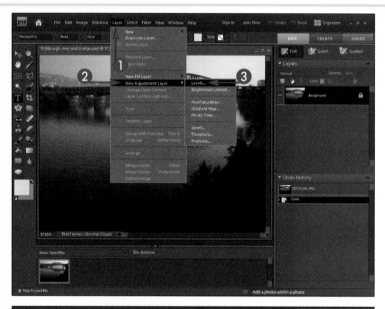

① Click Layer.

② Select New Adjustment Layer.

③ Choose Levels.

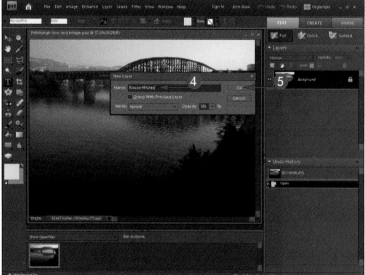

A New Layer dialog box opens.

④ Change the layer's name to **Blacks-Whites** by typing it into the Name box.

Leave the rest of the options alone and go with the defaults.

⑤ Click OK.

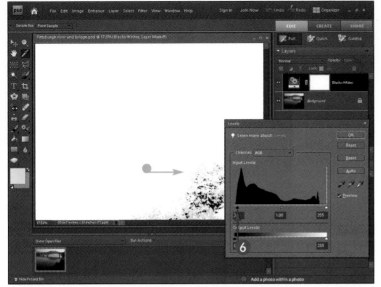

The Levels dialog box opens; it looks identical to the dialog box that you open from the Adjust Lighting option under the Enhance menu.

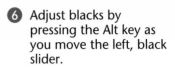

**DIFFICULTY LEVEL**

**6** Adjust blacks by pressing the Alt key as you move the left, black slider.

● A blacks threshold screen appears, showing you where the blacks are occurring as you adjust.

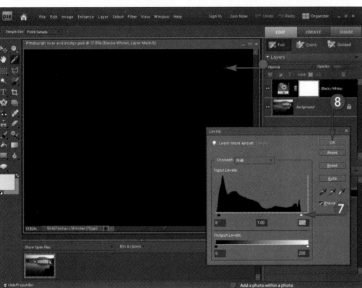

**7** Adjust whites by pressing the Alt key as you move the right, white slider.

● A whites threshold screen appears, showing you where the whites are occurring as you adjust.

**8** Click OK.

## TIPS

### Did You Know?

Threshold screens show you where certain tones appear in a picture. This is easy to figure out when the tones are either pure black or pure white. The colors show maxed-out channels. Use them when a picture is filled with color and a pure black or white is hard to find.

### Get Rid of Layers!

If you decide that the layer you are working on is messed up and you need to get rid of it, that is very easy to do. Simply click that layer and drag it up to the trash can icon at the top right of the Layers palette, just under the Opacity number.

### Did You Know?

The histogram, or graph, in Levels gives you an idea of what needs to be adjusted for blacks and whites. A big gap at either side means that no data is there, which translates as no tones. Most photographs look best when no big gap is on either side, which is what adjusting blacks and whites affects.

# WORK MIDTONES
## with a Levels adjustment layer

You started work on your photograph by adjusting blacks and whites with a Levels adjustment layer. You will now add another Levels adjustment layer to change the midtones. Photoshop Elements does not offer Color Curves as an adjustment layer, so you have to use Levels for midtones. Although Levels does not have as much control over midtones as Color Curves, it does offer a lot of flexibility when used as an adjustment layer.

Adjusting midtones is important because it affects the overall brightness or darkness of the picture. Do not use the black slider or white slider for this purpose, even though both seem to affect the overall brightness of the picture.

Name that Levels layer **Midtones** so that you can know exactly which layer is which simply by reading the names. If you follow a consistent workflow, the first layer will always be blacks and whites, and the second layer will be midtones.

① Click Layer.

② Select New Adjustment Layer.

③ Choose Levels.

A New Layer dialog box opens.

④ Change the layer's name to **Midtones** by typing it into the Name box.

⑤ Click OK.

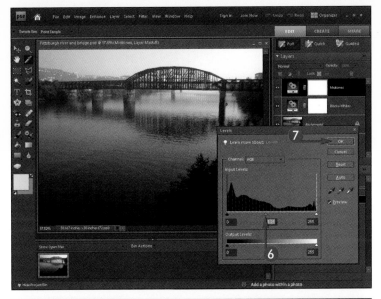

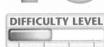

The Levels dialog box opens; it looks identical to the dialog box that you open from the Adjust Lighting option under the Enhance menu.

**6** Adjust midtones by moving the middle slider left or right.

The photograph and its midtones get brighter as you move the slider to the left.

The photograph and its midtones get darker as you move the slider to the right.

**7** Click OK.

● Two adjustment layers now sit on top of the original picture and affect how it looks.

**DIFFICULTY LEVEL**

## TIPS

### Try This!

Cropping is important when you are working with layers, too. You can crop at any time using the technique described in task #14. Cropping occurs across all of the layers and is a destructive form of processing, so limit your cropping at first to just getting rid of problems.

### Important!

Name your layers. You will find that this makes working with layers a lot easier as you begin to add more layers during the process. It can get confusing as to which one is doing what. In addition, named layers can help you see the process used in working on the picture — simply look at the layers from the bottom to the top.

### Try This!

The Color Curves adjustment is a good one for midtones, but it is not available as an adjustment layer. Often you will find that your blacks/whites Levels adjustment is pretty standard and can be applied directly to the pixels of your picture. That way you can use the Color Curves for midtones and use adjustment layers for the rest of your image processing.

# CORRECT COLOR
## with an adjustment layer

Color casts can be a problem with any type of photography. *Color casts* are those subtle colors that creep into an image and contaminate the colors and tones throughout the photograph. This can mean bluish landscapes at sunrise, greenish hair, and so on. They were a serious problem when everyone shot film because they could be hard to get rid of. With digital photography, correcting color by removing problem color casts has become a lot easier.

When you correct color with an adjustment layer, you gain a great deal of flexibility. If you decide that a previous color correction was not quite right as you continue to work on a photograph, you can always reopen the adjustment and do it again. That is always a great advantage of the nondestructive nature of adjustment layers. In addition, you can use the opacity of the layer to change how strongly the adjustment affects the photograph.

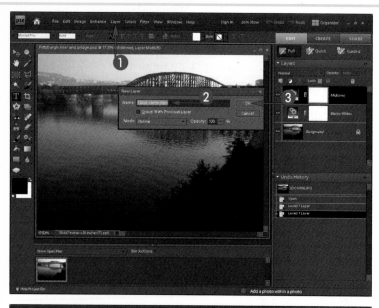

1 Click Layer, click New Adjustment Layer, and click Levels.

2 Change the layer's name to **Color correction** by typing it into the Name box.

3 Click OK.

4 Click the middle eyedropper in Levels.

5 Move the cursor into the picture and click something that should be a neutral white, gray, or black.

This removes a color cast from a neutral tone every time you click.

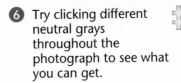

## 47

**DIFFICULTY LEVEL**

⑥ Try clicking different neutral grays throughout the photograph to see what you can get.

Sometimes you can get the right color on the first click, and sometimes it takes a number of clicks.

⑦ Click OK.

If you like the overall color, but it is too strong, you can change the Opacity of the layer.

⑧ Position your cursor over the word *Opacity*.

The cursor changes to a hand with arrows.

⑨ Click and drag left and right to change the opacity of the layer.

---

**TIPS**

### Did You Know?
Opacity is the opposite of transparency. Both of these terms refer to how much you can see through something, a layer in this case. Lower opacity for adjustment layers means that the layers lose some of their adjustments' strength.

### Important!
The first layers in the workflow described here are all Levels. Although all the adjustments could be made in one Levels control, this would give you a lot less flexibility. By separating the adjustments into separate layers, you can adjust each control individually. This means you can also readjust each control individually.

### Did You Know?
As you make more adjustments with Levels, and sometimes with other controls, you will find gaps begin to appear in the histogram in Levels. These are not necessarily a problem. They become a problem only when tonalities such as gradations in your photograph start to break up. This breakup will be very obvious, looking like steps where there are none, for example.

---

**Chapter 5: Create Adjustment Layers for Nondestructive Changes**

# ENHANCE COLOR
## with an adjustment layer

Colors in a photograph often need to be enhanced. The camera simply is not capable of seeing colors in the world the same way that we do. Sometimes the camera and sensor capture colors that have an unpleasant color cast in them, the correction of which was discussed in the last task. Other times, the colors will be out of sync with what you saw of the scene — that could be colors stronger or weaker than what you envisioned for the photograph.

Many times, you need to give a slight boost to the color to make the picture livelier or more dramatic. All of these things can be done with a Hue/Saturation adjustment layer. You use this control the same way that was shown in Chapter 2.

In this task, you will learn a different way of opening an adjustment layer and renaming it.

❶ Click Adjustment Layer icon in the Layers palette.

A drop-down menu appears.

❷ Select Hue/Saturation.

The Hue/Saturation dialog box appears along with a new adjustment layer.

❸ Click and drag the Saturation slider to the right to increase saturation between 5 and 15 points as needed.

④ Click the Edit drop-down menu and select a specific color to adjust.

⑤ Move the Saturation slider to the right as needed.

You can increase saturation more when you work with individual colors and still avoid problems.

⑥ Click OK.

## 48

DIFFICULTY LEVEL

⑦ Double-click the original Hue/Saturation label for the layer.

⑧ Type a new name, **Enhance colors**.

---

## TIPS

### Caution!

When working with Hue/Saturation, be careful that you do not oversaturate colors. This can make the picture look garish and unattractive very quickly. It is tempting to increase the saturation of your picture to make the colors look bright and lively, but this can also create a harsh quality for the image.

### More Options!

You can readjust the palette bin to make it display the layers in your Layers palette better. For example, the Undo History palette does not need as much space as the Layers palette often does. You can click and drag the dividing line between these palettes to make them smaller or larger.

### Did You Know?

You can change the size of the layers in the Layers palette. You may want them bigger so that the icon appears larger. Do this by clicking the double arrows at the top of the palette, then go to the bottom of that drop-down menu and select Palette Options. This gives you choices for the size of layers.

---

# FIX PROBLEM EXPOSURES
## with layer blending modes

At times your picture may be simply too dark or too light. There are many reasons why this can happen. Sometimes the camera makes a mistake in exposure, or sometimes the photographer sets the camera wrong. Regardless, you end up with a picture that needs immediate correction, either making it brighter or making it darker.

Photoshop Elements gives you an interesting tool to do this in its layer blending modes. You need to add an adjustment layer to your photograph. It really

does not matter which adjustment you choose because you will not be using the adjustment layer for its original adjustment purpose. You are simply using this layer so that Photoshop Elements has something to work with when communicating between layers, which is what layer blending modes do. When you first open the blending modes, you see a long list — ignore those choices and concentrate on two key modes for photographers, Multiply and Screen.

### FIX A TOO-BRIGHT PHOTOGRAPH

**1** Click Adjustment Layer icon and select Levels.

**2** Click OK without making any adjustments.

● The new adjustment layer appears in the Layers palette.

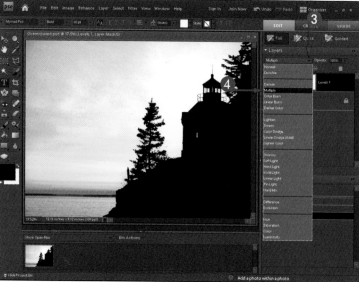

**3** Click the blending modes drop-down menu, which says Normal by default.

**4** Click Multiply.

The whole photo darkens by about one f-stop.

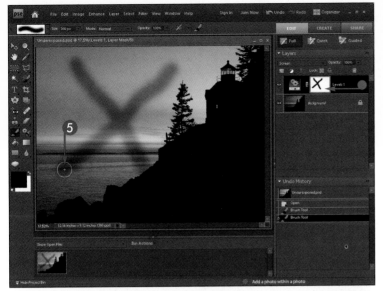

**⑤** Click and paint two lines across your picture to create an X.

● A black X now appears in the layer mask icon.

You did not draw a black X on the picture, but in the layer mask.

This black X in the layer mask then blocks the original adjustment which creates the effect in the picture.

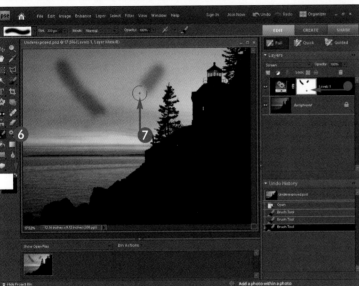

**⑥** Click the curved arrow between the foreground and background colors so that white is on top.

**⑦** Paint out the X in your photograph by painting white over the black.

● This removes the black which then allows the effect of the adjustment layer to reappear.

**TIPS**

### Important!
Layer masks affect what a layer does but not the actual adjustment. This is an important distinction. Putting black in a layer mask might block a darkening effect and make the picture brighter, or it could block a brightening effect and make the picture darker. You have to think in terms of black blocking an effect and not creating its own effect.

### Practice!
Layer masks can be counterintuitive for the photographer. Yet they are an extremely important tool to understand. You can do it! It just takes practice. You have to add adjustment layers with different sorts of controls and then paint in black and white to see how the layer mask works by blocking or allowing those adjustments.

### Patience!
Be patient with yourself as you learn to use layer masks. Photographers often get frustrated with this feature of Photoshop Elements because it often does not make sense right away. But once you start using layer masks, you will find that their value is so great that learning them is worth the effort.

# REMOVE ADJUSTMENTS
## with black

Once you start working with layer masks, you will learn the real power of adjustment layers. It is very common to do early adjustments such as setting blacks and whites in a picture and run into a problem with the range of tones. For example, to adjust most of the whites in the picture properly, you may find there is one small area in a photograph that gets overadjusted for that area. If you try to adjust Levels for that one white, then the rest of the picture does not get the proper adjustment.

Fortunately, you have a layer mask associated with every adjustment layer. You can make the correct adjustment for the overall picture and ignore what happens with one small part such as that small area of white. You simply use a black brush and paint over that problem part of the picture. That blocks the adjustment and gives you much more control over your picture.

**Note:** *Open a photo that has a contrast challenge with something very bright.*

● In this photo, the midtones make the goalie look okay, but the player in white and the grass are too bright.

① Choose the Paintbrush from the toolbox.

② If black is not the foreground color, click the curved arrow between the foreground and background colors so that black is on top.

③ Right-click the picture to get the brush size menu and choose a brush size appropriate to the problem.

④ Paint black over the problem to block the adjustment.

● The layer adjustment icon indicates the painted area.

# 51

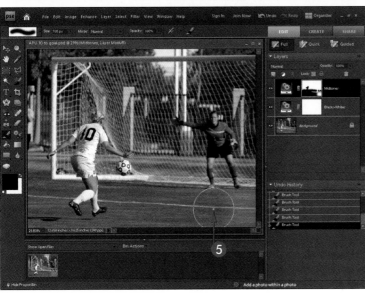

⑤ Change your brush size as needed to block or allow the adjustment in other areas.

---

**TIPS**

### More Options!

You can change how strong the blocking effect of black is, or the effect of white, by changing the Opacity of the brush. This is adjusted in the options bar above the photograph. A number of options are here for affecting how a brush works.

### Remember This!

As you gain experience working on layer masks, you will discover that you are constantly changing the brush size to match the needs of your photograph. Remember that this is easy to do by using the bracket keys to the right of the letter P — [ to make the brush smaller and ] to make it larger.

### Important!

Once you start working with more than one adjustment layer, you have to be sure you are in the right layer and layer mask. It can be frustrating and confusing if you start painting in the wrong layer mask. To be sure, you can simply click the layer mask icon in the correct layer in the Layers palette. The correct layer is also highlighted in black.

---

# ADD ADJUSTMENTS
## using black and then white

Sometimes you will run into a photograph that simply needs an adjustment in one area but not in the rest of the image. You could try adjusting the whole picture and then block out everything in the picture, doing a lot of work with a black paintbrush. If there really is only a small area that needs to be adjusted, that can be a lot of work.

There is a better way. You first make the adjustment as best you can for the small area that needs the change. You ignore what happens in the rest of the photograph. Then you block the entire adjustment by filling the entire layer mask with black. Next you take a white paintbrush and bring the adjustment back in only the areas where you want it. Essentially you are adding an adjustment to a very specific area without affecting the entire picture.

IDENTIFY THE PROBLEM

❶ Open a photo that has a small area that needs adjustment compared to the rest of the picture.

In this photo, the overall desert scene looks fine, but the mountains and sky in the distance are washed out.

❷ Add an adjustment that will correct the problem area even though it makes the whole picture look wrong.

● A Levels adjustment layer was added to this photo without adjustment.

● Then the Multiply mode was chosen.

The top of the photo looks much better now, but the rest of the picture is too dark.

120

## ADD BLACK

1 Click Edit.

2 Select Fill Layer.

DIFFICULTY LEVEL

The Fill Layer dialog box appears.

3 Click the Use drop-down menu and select Black.

Leave the other options at their defaults.

4 Click OK.

## TIPS

### More Options!

Often you need to switch back and forth between black and white as you work on the layer mask. This makes it easy to block or unblock an effect from an adjustment layer. You can quickly and easily change your brush color by using the X key to switch between black and white.

### More Options!

You may be working on a picture and find that the layer mask gets confusing. You cannot tell what you have or have not done. To start with a clean slate, you can fill the layer mask with white by using the Fill Layer under the Edit menu but choosing white instead of black.

### Try This!

When working with the Multiply or Screen blending modes, you may find that the first use of the mode helps but is not enough. If you duplicate this layer, you can increase the effect even more. Duplicate the layer by dragging it to the New Layer icon (🗔), which is to the left of the Adjustment Layer icon (◪).

# ADD ADJUSTMENTS
## using black and then white

A common problem in photographs is a lack of balance among the tones. The camera wants to interpret the scene very differently than your eyes do. You can see all of the detail from bright to dark areas just fine, but the camera cannot. In order to bring that picture back to balance, you do need to make some adjustments in Photoshop Elements.

This is where layer masks really shine. You can very carefully choose exactly what areas of the picture are going to be affected by any individual adjustment. That can either mean blocking an overadjustment or allowing a small area of a very specific adjustment as is seen here. You will sometimes hear people say that this is "cheating." That comes from a lack of understanding of how photography really works. You should be able to control your picture to interpret it closer to what you really saw.

● The photo now has a Multiply adjustment layer, but its effect is blocked by the black in the layer mask.

The picture looks as if no Multiply adjustment has been made at all.

ADJUST THE WHITES

**1** Select the Paintbrush tool.

**2** Change the foreground color to white.

**3** Change your brush size to match the area that needs to be adjusted.

**4** Paint the brush with the white foreground color over the area that needs to be changed.

The adjustment is now allowed, but only in that area.

**5** Change the foreground color to black.

**6** Make a smaller brush.

**7** Paint over problems along the edge between adjusted and unadjusted areas.

The black brush now blocks the adjustment again to fix the edge.

## TIPS

### Important!

Generally you will want to use soft-edged brushes for the layer mask. Soft brushes allow you to better blend the adjusted and the unadjusted areas. Hard-edged brushes can cause problems by making your brush lines show up. Use them sparingly.

### More Options!

Selections can be used in a layer mask. This can be important if you want to adjust something to a very tight edge. It is better to make a selection and paint black or white right up along the edge of the selection instead of trying to use a hard-edged brush. This gives you a better edge. See task #53 for more about selections.

### Important!

Edges are very important. One thing that often gives away a poorly adjusted image is the edge between an adjusted and unadjusted area. Pay close attention to what is happening along that edge. Use smaller brushes for a tight edge or larger brushes for a soft edge. And when you have a very tight edge, use a selection, even changing the feathering.

# COMBINE LAYER MASKS
## with selections

Everything you learned about selections still applies when working with adjustment layers and layer masks. Sometimes it is easier to simply paint an effect on or off the picture by using white or black, but other times your workflow is made more efficient by creating a selection first. When you create a selection and then add an adjustment layer, a layer mask is automatically created for you based on that selection.

A selection limits an effect to one area and blocks the effect outside that area. A layer mask limits an effect to an area controlled by white and blocks the effect where the mask is black. Making a selection then adding an adjustment layer creates a layer mask with white as the selected area and black outside the selection. Selections can be very helpful when very specific areas need to be adjusted, such as creating dark edges for a photograph.

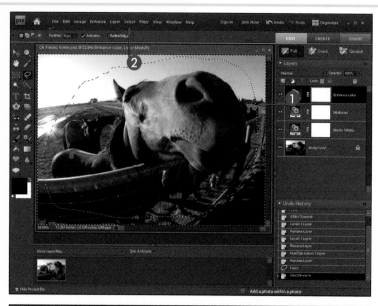

**1** Make a selection around the subject, inside the outer edges.

**2** Invert the selection by clicking Select and then Inverse.

**3** Open a Brightness/Contrast adjustment layer from the icon in the Layers palette.

**4** Reduce Brightness to about –30.

● The layer mask is controlling the effect, but the edge is very sharp and unattractive.

**5** Click OK.

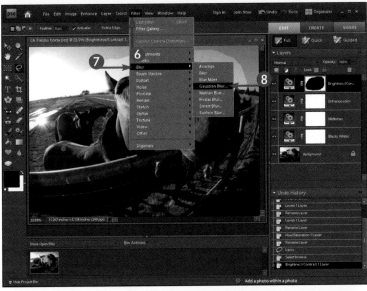

**6** Click Filter.

**7** Select Blur.

**8** Select Gaussian Blur.

## 53

**DIFFICULTY LEVEL**

**9** Click and drag the Radius slider to a high amount.

Depending on the photograph, this can be as low as 40 or as high as over 200.

**10** Click OK.

A soft darkness is applied to the outer edges of the photo.

---

 **TIPS**

### Did You Know?

Using Gaussian Blur for blending edges has a lot of advantages over using feathering with selections. Feathering must be done to a specific number, and then you click OK and look to see if the effect is what you want. With Gaussian Blur and a layer mask, you can change the Radius and watch the blending occur in real time.

### More Options!

When you first open Gaussian Blur, you might not see the edge to be blurred in the preview box. Simply move your cursor out into the picture and click the edge. That immediately places the black-white edge inside the preview box so you can see what happens as Gaussian Blur is increased.

### Important!

A great advantage of adjustment layers is the ability to change the adjustment. In this edge-darkening technique, for example, you can always double-click the icon for the Brightness/Contrast adjustment layer and reopen the adjustment dialog box. You can then change that edge darkness as desired.

---

**Chapter 5: Create Adjustment Layers for Nondestructive Changes**

# BALANCE COLORS AND TONES
## in a picture

A common challenge photographers face is a picture that is not balanced visually to match the composition or the way that people really see a subject. If you look at a scene, for example, your eye balances out the brightness levels so that you can easily see and compare elements of that scene. The camera does no such thing. If the left side of a scene is brighter than the right, the camera shows it just that way, creating an imbalance in the tones of the picture compared to

the way you see the scene. Colors can have a similar problem when one color starts to dominate the picture because it is too saturated compared to the others.

Through the use of adjustment layers and layer masks, you can fix this imbalance and help your photographs communicate something much closer to what you originally saw when you took the picture.

❶ Click the Adjustment Layer icon to open a Levels adjustment layer to correct an imbalance in brightness.

❷ Adjust the sliders until the problem area looks better.

● Ignore what happens in the rest of the photo because it will be overadjusted.

## 54

**3** Select the Gradient tool from the toolbox.

**4** Choose your foreground/background colors to be black and white.

**5** Click your cursor in the area where you want to block your adjustment.

**6** Drag your cursor into the area where you want to keep the adjustment.

● The gradient tool puts black in the first area, white in the second area, and creates a blend between them.

The image now has its tonalities better blended.

---

 **TIPS**

### Did You Know?

If you get the white and black parts of the gradient tool mixed up, do not worry. That is actually a common challenge when first learning to use the Gradient tool. If you click and drag and the black and white show up in the wrong places, simply do it again in the reverse direction.

### More Options!

You may need to do multiple applications of the Gradient tool before the picture looks right. Sometimes the angle will be wrong, other times the gradient will be too short and too obvious, and other times the gradient will be too long and ineffective. Keep trying until your picture looks right.

### Important!

Change the adjustment as needed after you use the Gradient tool. Sometimes you will guess wrong as to the correct amount of adjustment to properly balance the picture. When you apply the Gradient tool, the picture may look too dark or too light. Simply reopen that adjustment layer and readjust as needed.

---

# BRING OUT SHADOW DETAIL
## in specific areas

As you look to balance a picture's tonalities, you often discover small areas that are too dark. These are typically shadows that did not get the same light as the rest of the picture. Yet for the picture to really look right, for it to be interpreted closer to the way you saw a scene, these dark areas need to be increased in brightness.

Once again the adjustment layer and its layer mask come to the rescue. You use a blending mode again,

Screen, to brighten the dark area, and then you use the layer mask to limit that change just to the area needed. Although this works very well, one thing you may notice occurring is an increase in noise in those dark areas. There is nothing you can do about that. Revealing detail in dark areas often means revealing the noise that is there as well.

1 Open a Levels adjustment layer from the Adjustment Layer icon in the Layers palette.

2 Click OK without making any adjustments.

3 Click the layer blending modes drop-down menu.

4 Select Screen.

The lightening effect of Screen is applied to the whole picture.

⑤ Open the Fill Layer dialog box from the Edit menu.

⑥ Choose Black in the Use drop-down menu in Contents.

⑦ Click OK.

The lightening effect of Screen is blocked.

⑧ Select the Paintbrush from the toolbox.

⑨ Choose a brush size appropriate to the area being adjusted.

⑩ Choose white for the foreground color.

⑪ Paint in the lightening effect.

● The levels adjustment icon indicates the painted area.

# TIPS

## Important!
Edges are critical when you are dealing with small areas of change in a photograph and using a layer mask. A sloppily painted edge is very obvious in the picture and distracts the viewer even to the point of the truth of your picture coming into question.

## Apply It!
Work your edges by going back and forth between white and black brushes. In addition, change the size of your brushes by using the bracket keys as you go. If you are really having trouble with an edge, try using a selection to control where the black and white go within your layer mask.

## More Options!
You can actually see your layer mask in black and white over your photograph. Position your cursor over the layer mask icon in the layer you are working on. Press the Alt key as you click the layer mask icon and the layer mask will appear where your picture is. Press Alt and click again to get back to your picture.

# DARKEN HIGHLIGHT DETAIL
## in specific areas

As you continue to balance a picture's tonalities, you often find too-bright areas. These are typically highlight areas that received more light than your subject. When you expose properly for the subject, your photograph will look good where the subject is but these highlight areas will look overexposed. Once again, for the picture to look right, such out-of-balance bright areas need to be balanced, this time brought down in tone.

You use the adjustment layer and its layer mask again, but this time using the Multiply blending mode to darken the right area. The layer mask is used to limit that change just to the area needed. Luckily, no noise problems can come from darkening a bright area, but there are limits as to how much darkening you can do if the area is too overexposed.

① Open a Levels adjustment layer from the Adjustment Layer icon in the Layers palette.

② Click OK without making any adjustments.

③ Click the layer blending modes drop-down menu.

④ Select Multiply.

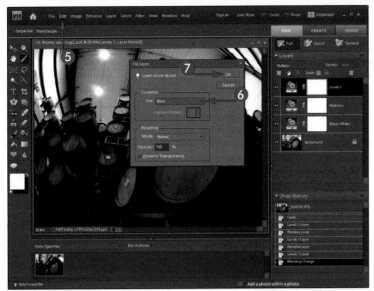

The darkening effect of Multiply is applied to the whole picture.

**5** Open the Fill Layer dialog box from the Edit menu.

**6** Choose Black in the Use drop-down menu in Contents.

**7** Click OK.

# 56

**DIFFICULTY LEVEL**

The darkening effect of Multiply is blocked.

**8** Select the Paintbrush from the toolbox.

**9** Choose a brush size appropriate to the area being adjusted.

**10** Choose white for the foreground color.

**11** Paint in the darkening effect.

● The levels adjustment icon indicates the painted area.

---

**TIPS**

### Important!

Exposure is very important when dealing with bright and highlight areas in a photograph. If a bright area is too washed out, no amount of work in Photoshop Elements will bring in any detail. When bright areas in a picture absolutely have to have detail, they must be captured when you take the picture.

### Did You Know?

Sometimes when you make a correction to a specific area in the photograph, the whole photograph changes in its appearance, maybe looking overall too bright or too dark. You can simply go back to your midtones adjustment layer, reopen the adjustment, and make a correction.

### More Options!

You do not have to limit your adjustments to simply fixing a bright area or a dark area. If your photograph needs help in both areas, then use two different adjustment layers, one set to Multiply and one set to Screen, and then use the layer masks appropriately to fix both places.

---

**Chapter 5: Create Adjustment Layers for Nondestructive Changes**

# Add a
# GRADUATED FILTER EFFECT

Skies can be a bold and beautiful part of an outdoor photograph, yet skies are often much different in brightness compared to the ground. Skies often look a lot better in real life than they do in a photograph, which is generally due to the out-of-balance way the camera sees the world compared to the way people do. When the sky is brought into balance with the rest of the picture, photographs often come alive and

much better express the feelings the photographer had when he or she originally took picture.

Many photographers use a filter called a *graduated neutral density filter* that allows them to darken the sky without darkening the ground. If you have good detail in the sky, you can mimic this effect in Photoshop Elements to get a more dramatic sky and a better interpretation of your scene.

**1** Open a Levels adjustment layer from the Adjustment Layer icon in the Layers palette.

**2** Click OK without making any adjustments.

**3** Click the layer blending modes drop-down menu.

**4** Select Multiply.

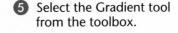

The darkening effect of Multiply is applied to the whole picture.

**5** Select the Gradient tool from the toolbox.

**6** Choose white for the foreground color.

**7** Click your cursor in the middle part of the sky.

**8** Drag your cursor down to the ground.

**DIFFICULTY LEVEL**

● The effect of the Multiply layer is now applied only to the sky at its maximum effect.

● The levels adjustment icon indicates the painted area.

● The effect blends very naturally with the use of the gradient tool down to the ground.

## TIPS

### Important!
The key to this technique for creating a graduated filter effect is in the blend, the distance of the gradient. If the picture does not look right, especially if there is too hard an edge between the dark and the light areas, reapply your gradient with a bigger distance between the starting and ending points.

### Try This!
After you apply your gradient and make the sky look good, you may discover there are some areas in the ground that look too bright. Simply take a white brush and brush over those areas so that you can allow the darkening effect of the Multiply mode on those areas as well.

### Try This!
One challenge with this technique is that the gradient can cover tall objects that extend into the sky from the ground. This could never be corrected with a graduated filter over a lens. You can correct it in Photoshop Elements by using a black paintbrush to paint over these objects and block the darkening effect.

# FLATTEN LAYERS
## when done

After working on your photo, you will come to the point where you are more or less done with it. You can save and store this photo as is, using a Photoshop PSD file, and keep all of its layers. Sometimes, however, you may want a simpler file that can be quickly used for other purposes than adjusting a picture. The PSD file format is not generally recognized outside of Adobe programs.

At this point it is a good idea to flatten the image, merging the layers together into a simplified image file, and then save the picture in the appropriate format. If you are going to use a photo for the Web or e-mail, choose a JPEG file. If you are preparing pictures for use in a brochure or other publication, you might decide to use a TIFF file. Flattening an image can be done through the Layer menu or through the Layers palette menu.

### USE THE MENU TO FLATTEN
① Click Layer.
② Select Flatten Image.

### USE THE PALETTE MENU TO FLATTEN
① Click the double arrows at the right of Layers.

A drop-down menu appears.

② Click Flatten Image.

● All layers and their effects are now merged.

SAVE THE FLATTENED IMAGE

① Click File.

② Select Save As.

The Save As dialog box appears.

Choose the appropriate file format, change the file name and folder location if needed, then click OK.

## TIPS

### Did You Know?

Some photographers save all of their layered files forever, just in case they want to revise the pictures. Other photographers find that saving all these layered files can get to be unwieldy and unnecessary for their workflow. There is no arbitrary right or wrong to this. It depends entirely on how comfortable you are with your work.

### Important!

Once your file is flattened and closed, you have no access to the original layers. If you flatten the file, you can always undo that in the Undo History palette if the picture is still open. But if an image is flattened and closed, that opportunity is gone and the layers are gone as well.

### Try This!

You can combine all of your layers and their effects into a single layer on top of the layer stack so that you have access to a "flattened file" and layers at the same time. Click the top layer and then press these keys: Ctrl+Shift+Alt+E. This merges the layers and then creates a new layer with that image on top of the layer stack.

# Solve Photo Problems

You always want to take the best possible picture when you squeeze the shutter on your camera. You do not want to have to fix problems in the picture that could have been corrected if the picture were taken more carefully from the start. Yet, no matter how hard you work, sooner or later you are going to have some problems in a photograph to fix.

These can be all sorts of things, ranging from dust on the sensor to unwanted light flare to blank skies and more. These are not anyone's fault, but things that crop up into a picture due to many factors, and keep that picture from being all that it can be. Sometimes these

problems are extremely annoying and very distracting to a viewer. At other times, they are a frustration mainly to the photographer. Regardless, you want them out of your picture.

Photoshop Elements has some excellent tools to deal with problems in the picture after you have done your basic processing. Some of them do take some time and practice to master, however. Do not be discouraged if you try something like the Clone tool and your results are not perfect at first. With practice and experience, you can master any tool in Photoshop Elements.

# Top 100

# CLONE OUT
## problems

*Cloning* works essentially by copying a small part of the picture from one area and then pasting that copy onto a new location in the photograph. This is done without you having to think about copying or pasting. It is simplified so that all you have to do is select a spot to copy from and a place to copy over. You tell Photoshop Elements where you want the cloning to start from, how big of a copy you want to make, and where to place the copy.

You set a "clone-from" point by pressing Alt as you click over the good part of the photo. You tell Photoshop Elements how big of a copy you want to make by the size you choose for your brush. Finally, you simply click multiple times over your problem area, and the program knows where to place the little copy of the picture area under the clone-from point.

① Click the Zoom tool, or magnifier, at the top of the toolbox.

② Click and drag your cursor around the problem area to magnify it.

③ Click the New Layer icon in the Layers palette.

● This creates a new, empty layer.

④ Name the layer *Clone layer*.

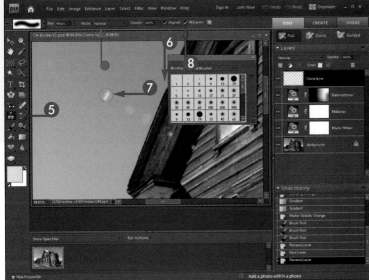

**5** Click the Clone Stamp tool in the toolbox.

**6** Right-click the photograph to open the brush menu that allows you to quickly select a specific size of brush.

**7** Pick a brush size appropriate to the problem.

● Keep Mode at Normal, Opacity 100%, and Aligned checked.

**8** Check All Layers (■ changes to ☑).

**9** Press Alt as you click an area near your problem, but a problem-free area.

This sets the clone-from point.

---

## TIPS

### Did You Know?

For most cloning, you will use the Aligned option for the cloning tool. This keeps the clone-from point of a line at the same distance and angle to your clone-to point as you clone. If your clone-from area is very small, uncheck Aligned so that the clone-from point always goes back to that area.

### Try This!

If you run into trouble with the settings of any tool, including the Clone Stamp tool, you can quickly reset the tool back to its defaults. Click the small down arrow at the far left of the options toolbar over the toolbox. This gives you a menu with the reset option. Usually you can just choose Reset Tool.

### Try This!

Once you magnify the area where you are cloning, you may need to adjust the position of that area slightly. If you press the spacebar, the cursor changes to a hand icon. Keep pressing the spacebar and then click and drag the picture to move it around. This works with any tool in Photoshop Elements.

# CLONE OUT
## problems

A common problem comes from *lens flare*, little light spots and circles going in a line away from where the sun would be in your picture, or where the sun is just outside of the picture frame. They can be very annoying and distracting. Other problems can include people inadvertently getting into the edge of the frame or a misplaced piece of trash in the picture.

The Clone Stamp tool is a very powerful way of covering up such problems. The keys to using this tool include cloning to a blank layer, clicking as you go for each clone spot rather than brushing continuously, resetting your clone-from point whenever you see problems, and changing your brush size as you go. By doing these things, your cloning will look more natural, without repeating patterns called *cloning artifacts*.

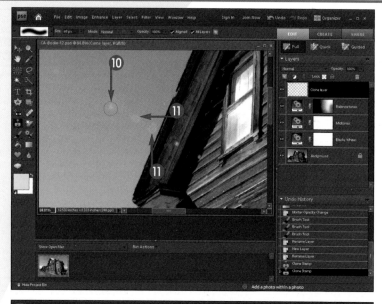

**10** Click over the problem area.

Click multiple times to cover the problem.

Change your clone-from point to keep the clone work blending.

**11** Continue to click over the problem areas.

Because you are on a layer, there is no problem if your cloning goes too far.

**12** If it does, click the Eraser tool.

**13** Right-click the image to get the brush menu and choose a small brush size.

**14** Erase the problem from the layer.

There is no effect on the rest of the photo.

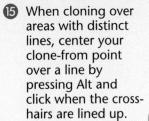

**# 59 CONTINUED**

⑮ When cloning over areas with distinct lines, center your clone-from point over a line by pressing Alt and click when the cross-hairs are lined up.

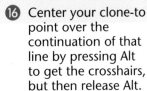

⑯ Center your clone-to point over the continuation of that line by pressing Alt to get the crosshairs, but then release Alt.

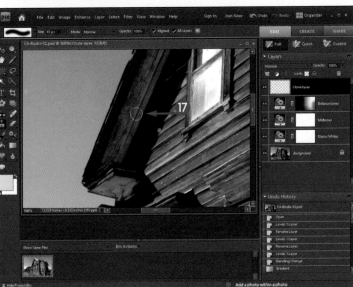

⑰ Click and clone over the problem.

The lines should line up.

If they do not line up, undo the work and reset the clone-from and clone-to points.

---

**TIPS**

**Try This!**

If the cloning starts looking messy, just take the Eraser tool and erase the work. Because you are working to a layer, you are only erasing something applied over the actual picture. You can always turn the visibility of the layer on and off to see this by clicking the eye icon at the left side of the layer.

**Important!**

To do cloning well takes practice. At first, it takes some time as you continually change your clone-from point and even your brush size so that the cloning blends well. It is important to do this because poorly done cloning draws attention to itself very quickly.

**Did You Know?**

Dust spots in the sky from sensor dust can be cleaned up using the Spot Healing Brush (🖌). This tool is in the group of tools just above the eraser. With it, you simply click the dust spot and Photoshop Elements copies something nearby over that spot and helps it blend. You can also use this tool with layers — check All Layers in the options bar.

# REMOVE PEOPLE FROM A SCENE
## with Photomerge

The United States has so many wonderful places to visit. These places attract a lot of people as well. That often means that photographing in some areas without people getting into your shot can be difficult.

Sometimes you can wait until a gap occurs in the flow of the crowd so that you get a picture without people. But often you cannot, especially if you are traveling with family who want to move on and see the other sights of the area.

Photoshop Elements now has a new feature that allows you to remove people from a scene. You have to shoot multiple pictures of that scene so that the people walking through it are not all in one place. You also need to shoot from the same position and hold your camera as steady as possible so that the overall framing of your picture does not change much.

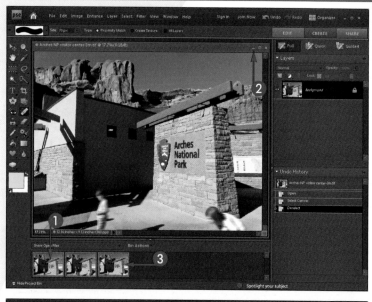

① Open the series of photos you need to clean up into the Project Bin.

② If they all open to the workspace, click the Minimize button to minimize them to the Project Bin.

③ Select the whole group by clicking the first photo, then pressing Shift as you click the last photo.

④ Click File.

⑤ Select New.

⑥ Choose Photomerge Scene Cleaner.

The Photomerge Scene Cleaner opens.

- A how-to panel also appears.

**7** Drag the best photo of your group into the Final photo window.

**8** Drag a different picture into the Source window.

**9** Click the Pencil tool in the how-to panel.

**10** Draw around the object you want to remove in the Final frame.

**11** Draw around an area in the Source window that you want to move to the Final frame.

Photomerge moves parts of the Source photo appropriately to the Final photo.

**12** Click Done when you are finished.

The photo opens into Full Edit with layers holding the work you did.

**TIPS**

### Did You Know?
Photoshop Elements includes some pretty amazing alignment work in its Photomerge feature. In order to match everything in the Scene Cleaner, the picture elements within the scene must line up. The program analyzes the pictures and lines them up for you. It helps to keep the image frame lined up as best you can while you shoot.

### Try This!
The Scene Cleaner may not work immediately the way you want it to. Undo your work, and then try drawing around a different part of the picture, drawing tighter to an area, and drawing in both the Source and the Final images because you will get different results.

### Try This!
Once you are done using the Scene Cleaner, you may discover that the photograph still has some imperfections. Instead of trying to do it all over again in the Scene Cleaner, you may find it quicker and easier to simply use the Clone Stamp tool to make small corrections as needed.

# Fix problems due to
# LENS DISTORTION

Many photographers have discovered the benefits of large-range zooms that go from very wide angle to quite telephoto focal lengths, such as 18-200mm or 28-300mm. These offer a lot of focal-length options in one lens, making them ideal for travel as well as a convenient way of always being prepared for whatever your subject might be. Such lenses are available for digital SLRs, but they also come built into many advanced compact digital cameras.

Such extreme focal length changes in one lens, however, challenge lens manufacturers. Most of these lenses have something called *barrel distortion*, especially common when shot at wider focal lengths. This causes a curving outward of straight lines near the top, bottom, or sides of the photograph. You can correct this in Photoshop Elements in the Correct Camera Distortion filter, even though you are actually correcting lens distortion.

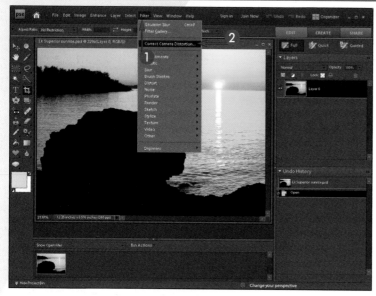

**1** Click Filter.

**2** Select Correct Camera Distortion.

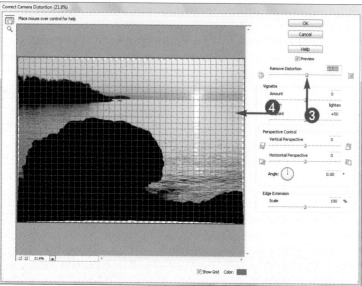

The Correct Camera Distortion window opens.

**3** Click the Remove Distortion slider and move it left or right to correct a curved horizon.

**4** Use the grid to help you determine when the line is straight.

144

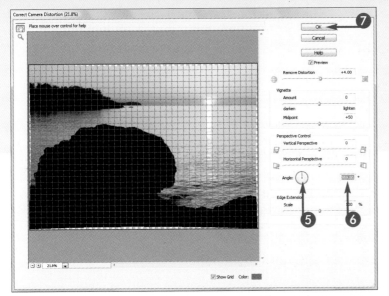

⑤ Correct any crooked horizons by clicking the Angle icon and dragging the pointer.

⑥ You can also correct crooked photos by typing a number in the angle degrees box.

⑦ When the photo is corrected, click OK.

DIFFICULTY LEVEL

● The photo opens into Full Edit with your work displayed as a single layer.

⑧ Select the Crop tool from the toolbox.

⑨ Use the Crop tool to crop out the distorted edges of the final picture.

⑩ Click the green check icon when you are finished.

## TIPS

### More Options!

The distorted edges that need cropping are often very close to the frame edge, and you will find it hard to move them without the crop edge snapping to the frame edge. Press Ctrl as you click and drag the crop edges in order to keep them from snapping to the frame edges.

### Try This!

Making these distortion corrections to a photograph results in gaps along the edges of your image. Those gaps are easy to fix with the Crop tool, but you can also try the Edge Extension slider in Correct Camera Distortion filter. This stretches edges and sometimes works, but it can make edges of the picture look funny, too.

### Try This!

The Vignette control in Correct Camera Distortion window is designed to correct uneven brightness from the center to the corners of the picture. Some lenses, especially wide-angle focal lengths of long-range zooms, darken the outside parts of the picture; such images can be corrected by using the Vignette sliders.

# FIX PERSPECTIVE PROBLEMS
## with building photographs

Buildings stand tall, but when you photograph them, they often look like they are falling over backwards. This is because when you get close to a building and point your camera up to photograph it, the camera and lens accentuate perspective so that the building appears smaller at the top than at the bottom. This is especially common with wide-angle focal lengths, and in the past, it took some very expensive gear to correct, which meant that architectural photography

was not as easy for the average photographer. In many situations, this weakens the look of the building. Correct Camera Distortion once again comes to the rescue for this fix. Although this is commonly used for buildings, it can also be used for tall trees, cliffs, and other tall objects. By straightening up these objects, they gain a very majestic look in your photograph.

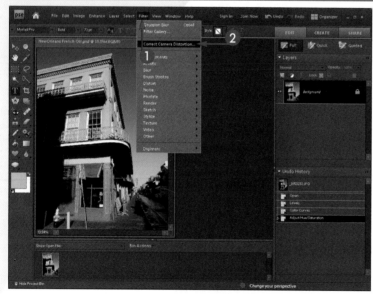

① Click Filter.

② Select Correct Camera Distortion.

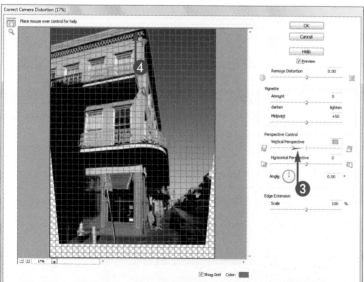

The Correct Camera Distortion window opens.

③ Click the Vertical Perspective slider and move it to the left to straighten up a building.

④ Use the grid to help you determine when the building is straight.

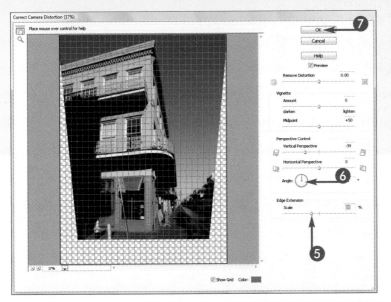

5 Use Edge Extension to bring back important parts of the picture.

6 Correct any left or right lean with the Angle control.

7 When the photo is corrected, click OK.

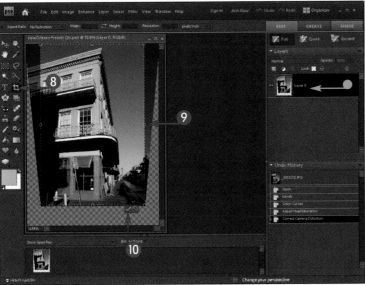

● The photo opens into Full Edit with your work displayed as a single layer.

8 Select the Crop tool from the toolbox.

9 Use the Crop tool to crop out the distorted edges of the final picture.

10 Click the green check icon when you are finished.

---

**TIPS**

### Did You Know?

In order to control perspective in the past, such as leaning buildings, photographers had to use special equipment. They would use perspective control lenses that allowed them to move the lens to get a whole building into the scene instead of tilting the camera. A view camera offered the same control.

### Try This!

As you adjust the perspective of your picture, you may find that you lose certain parts of the image. Often there is nothing you can do about that. In that case, use your Crop tool creatively. Instead of just trying to get everything into the picture, which cannot be done, crop your picture so that it looks interesting.

### Try This!

When you tilt the camera up at a tall building, perspective always makes it look like it is falling backward. If you use a very wide-angle lens and get very close to the building, this can be a dramatic effect and not something that you want to correct in Photoshop Elements.

# Make an
# OUT-OF-FOCUS BACKGROUND

A good background can really set your subject off nicely in a photo. But for a variety of reasons, sometimes you simply cannot take a picture of your subject in front of a great background. This can be especially true if you are taking a snapshot of family with a little point-and-shoot camera you just happened to have in your pocket.

One way of improving backgrounds is to make them out of focus. Sometimes you can do that when you

are taking the picture, but you can also blur the background behind your subject in Photoshop Elements. The latter action can actually give you more control over your background, although it can be a challenge to make it look right. Although you can use selections to blur a background, you will find your results come faster and look better when you use layers.

1 Click your flattened photo.

2 Press Ctrl+J twice to duplicate your layer twice.

● Duplicate layers appear over your original.

3 Click the top layer's eye icon to turn it off.

4 Click the middle layer to select it.

5 Click Filter.

6 Select Blur.

7 Choose Gaussian Blur.

The Gaussian Blur dialog box appears.

⑧ Click and drag the Radius slider until the background looks out of focus.

⑨ Ignore what is happening to the subject.

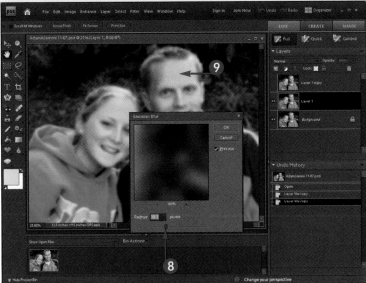

⑩ Click the top layer's eye icon to turn it back on.

⑪ Click the top layer to select it.

⑫ Click the Eraser tool in the toolbox.

⑬ Select a good size for the Eraser based on the area of the background.

⑭ Click and drag to erase the sharp parts of the top photo layer so the underlying blurred parts show through.

If you go too far, use the Undo History palette or Ctrl+Z to back up.

## TIPS

### Caution!
Be careful of the amount of blur used. Too much blur and the photo will look more surreal than real. Also, watch the edges as you erase. Edges can make or break this effect. Change your brush size and hardness as you go around important edges on your subject. You may also need a selection to protect an important edge.

### Try This!
If you want to keep your layers, you can use the merge and copy layers technique in the tips in Chapter 5. You need a flattened "photo," but a flattened layer representing that photo will do. Select the top layer and then press Ctrl+Shift+Alt+E to create a merged-flattened layer above it that can be used for this task.

### Try This!
You can also make a selection around your subject, feather it appropriately, and then press Delete or Backspace to reveal the background. On some photos, this gives better results, especially if the subject has a lot of intricate edge detail. On other photos, making a selection just takes more time, and the Eraser technique is more efficient and effective.

# Remove
# DISTRACTING COLORS

Color is important for most photographs. Color is not, however, arbitrary and constant. Any color is influenced by other colors around it, dark or bright areas near it, people's feelings about color, and how a particular sensor and camera deal with that color. Colors are never a constant.

One common problem comes from having a distracting color within the image area. This is probably most common with red. Red is a very dominant color and attracts the viewer's eye away from other parts of the picture. This is especially a problem if the subject does not have bright colors that can compete with it. Other colors can be a problem, too, especially when they are bright and saturated and draw attention away from the real action of the photo. Removing or at least toning down problem colors can be an important adjustment for your photograph.

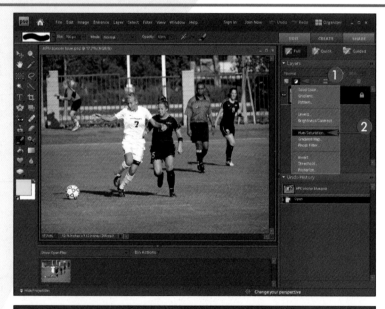

① Click the Adjustment Layer icon in the Layers palette.

② Select Hue/Saturation.

A Hue/Saturation adjustment layer is added to the picture, and the Hue/Saturation dialog box appears.

③ Click the Edit drop-down menu.

④ Select the color appropriate to the color you want to change in your photograph.

⑤ Position your cursor over that color in the picture and click the color to refine the Hue/Saturation adjustment limits.

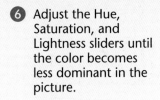 

**6** Adjust the Hue, Saturation, and Lightness sliders until the color becomes less dominant in the picture.

Usually, the Saturation slider is the most important, but try them all.

**7** Click OK.

**8** Press Ctrl+I to invert the white layer mask to black.

**9** Select the Paintbrush.

**10** Change the foreground color to white.

**11** Paint white over the problem color area.

This allows you to limit the color adjustment to only one part of the picture.

---

**TIPS**

### Did You Know?

You can change the layer mask between black and white in several ways. Use Ctrl+I to invert a color mask from white to black or black to white. Use the Edit menu and Fill Layer to completely fill the layer mask with black or white, which replaces any work done in the layer mask.

### Try This!

Use this technique to tone down a color in the background of your photograph that cannot be removed in any other way. You may find that you cannot crop that color out nor can you blur it without adversely affecting the rest of the picture. Yet, by simply toning it down, you make it less dominant.

### Try This!

If several colors are giving you problems, use a separate adjustment layer for each one. Although it is possible to do more than one color with a single adjustment layer, that can be confusing. Using single layers for each color makes it easy to go to the exact layer needed for any adjustment. Name your layers by the color affected.

# Improve
# BLANK SKIES

During the day, skies are bright. Typically, they are much brighter than anything on the ground. If you try to photograph the sky so that it has good color, you usually end up with a silhouette for a subject. If you expose to get good detail in the subject, then the sky becomes blank white. Another problem occurs when photographing on days with a hazy sky. The sky often looks blank in the photograph then as well.

You could select the sky and simply fill it with a blue. This usually does not look very good, even to the point of looking quite artificial. Skies are not a consistent shade of blue. They are darker higher in the sky, and get lighter closer to the horizon. This needs to be duplicated when fixing a blank sky so that it looks right.

① Click the Magic Wand selection tool.

② Click the sky to select it.

Shift-click multiple times as needed to get all of the sky.

③ Click the New Layer icon in the Layers palette to add a blank layer.

④ Rename your layer to Fix Sky.

⑤ Click Select and choose Refine Edge.

The Refine Edge dialog box appears.

⑥ Click the red icon to create an overlay to better show the edges of your selection.

⑦ Adjust Smooth, Feather, and Contract/Expand until the edges along the sky look good.

⑧ Click OK.

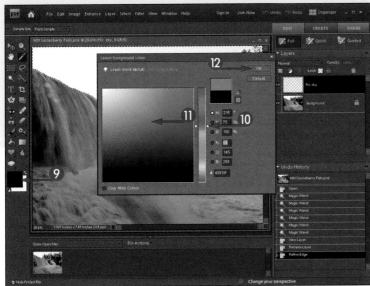
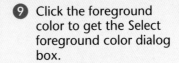
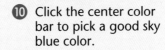

**#65**

**DIFFICULTY LEVEL**

**9** Click the foreground color to get the Select foreground color dialog box.

**10** Click the center color bar to pick a good sky blue color.

**11** Click in the big color box to refine that color pick.

**12** Click OK.

**13** Click the background color to get the Select background color dialog box.

**14** Click the center color bar to pick a good sky blue color.

**15** Click in the big color box to get a color lighter than the foreground color.

**16** Click OK.

---

**TIPS**

**Did You Know?**

Refine Edge is a useful control in Photoshop Elements for refining a selection edge. All of the controls in Refine Edge were possible before in Photoshop Elements, but they were not so convenient or so directly accessible. Being able to add an overlay that clearly shows what edges will look like based on the selection is also a great benefit.

**Try This!**

When you deal with skies that are broken up by the subject, by trees in the background, and other pictorial objects, you may find it helpful to use the Magic Wand with Contiguous unchecked. This allows the program to look for the sky throughout the picture even if it is not directly connected to the area that you click on.

**Did You Know?**

The color picker that appears when you click the foreground or background color allows you to choose all sorts of colors. The central color bar is for selecting hue. The large box allows you to select the brightness of a color from left to right and the saturation from top to bottom.

# Improve
# BLANK SKIES

Putting a sky fix into a separate layer over your picture has several advantages. It allows you to change and tweak the sky as much as you want without affecting the underlying picture. In addition, it allows you to tone down the intensity of the fixed colors by simply modifying the Opacity of the layer. You can also change the color of the sky by using Hue/Saturation on the layer.

Finally, a separate layer is very important because it allows you to add noise to the fixed sky. All photographs have some sort of noise at some level. When Photoshop Elements adds color, it adds it very pure, without any noise whatsoever. This can make the sky look unnatural, even though a real sky has no noise. You need to add some noise to the sky fix so that it matches the rest of the photograph.

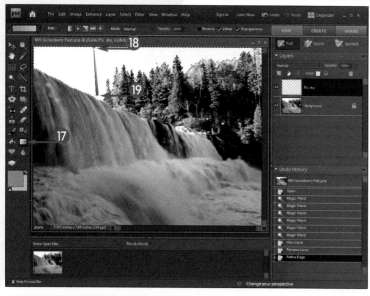

⑰ Click the Gradient tool.

⑱ Click high in the sky to start the gradient.

⑲ Drag your cursor down to the bottom of the sky and release to end the gradient.

A new sky appears; it will usually be too intense.

⑳ Deselect your selection by pressing the Esc key.

㉑ Adjust the Opacity of the sky layer until the sky looks natural.

㉒ Click the Zoom tool or magnifier, and then click the photo to enlarge it to a small section of sky in the original photo.

㉓ Click the Hand tool, and then click and drag your photo to get a good view of the noise in the original photo and the new sky.

㉔ Click Filter, Noise, and Add Noise.

The Add Noise dialog box opens.

㉕ Add a small amount of noise so the sky matches the original photo better.

---

## TIPS

### Caution!

Be sure you are in the right layer when you add the sky. You do not want to add the sky to the original image or to any other layer that you might be using. This will cause you problems, although of course you can undo them with the Undo History palette.

### Try This!

Often you will find that it takes several tries with the Gradient tool to get a good-looking gradient for sky. You may find that the sky looks crooked at one time, does not seem to match the way the rest of the scene looks at another, or the blend is too high or too low. Simply keep trying the tool until you get it looking good.

### More Options!

The Gradient tool has a number of options in the options bar. Most photographers use this tool at its default settings. However, some other interesting gradients can be chosen in the options bar. You might like experimenting with them for special-effect purposes. Use the Reset Tool function at the far left to get back to the defaults.

# CONCENTRATE ATTENTION
## with Gaussian Blur

Photographs look their best when the image is clearly structured for the viewer. You want the viewer to be able to understand what your picture is about or at least understand your interpretation of the scene. Composition, filters, depth of field, and other shooting techniques are used to help define and structure the picture so that it affects the viewer.

A trendy effect that photographers have been using for this purpose is a very special use of sharpness. By using special lenses, they create a small area of sharpness within the picture to define exactly what it is they want the viewer to look at. You can do something very similar in Photoshop Elements. You will be creating a blur over most of the picture that blends nicely to a sharp area. By choosing this sharp area carefully, you can create a very strong way of communicating to your viewer.

① Make a selection around a key part of your subject.

② Click Select and choose Feather.

③ Feather the selection by about 80 pixels.

④ Click Select.

⑤ Choose Inverse to invert the selection.

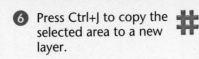 

6 Press Ctrl+J to copy the selected area to a new layer.

● You will see a layer with a hole in it over your original image.

**# 66**

7 Click Filter, Blur, and Gaussian Blur.

8 Click and drag the Radius slider until you get a nice blurred effect on the top layer.

The hole in the top layer allows the sharp photo underneath to show through only in that area.

---

 **TIPS**

### Try This!

You can refine your final picture by using the Eraser tool. Choose a soft-edged brush for the eraser and erase parts of the top blurred layer. Press Ctrl+Z to undo anything you do not like. You can also change the Opacity of the eraser to get a more blended effect as you erase an edge.

### Did You Know?

A checkerboard pattern on a layer thumbnail in the Layers palette shows you that no pixels are there. This pattern occurs only on pixel layers. This can help you know when a layer has holes or gaps in it so that you can choose the right layer to work on. It also gives you an idea of the shape of the hole.

### Try This!

If you are having trouble finding the edge of a layer's pixels as you erase on that layer, try turning off the layer below it. Click the eye icon to turn the layer off; that way you see only the layer you are working on. A checkerboard pattern shows up where the pixels are gone.

# ADD A NEW BACKGROUND
## for your subject

How often have you taken a picture of friends or family, and you have liked the subject but not the background? This happens all the time. Sometimes the liveliest photos that really give an interesting interpretation of the person are captured informally, even spur of the moment with a point-and-shoot camera. In these situations, you rarely have the chance to choose a great background for your subject.

It is possible to change the background in Photoshop Elements. You can create everything from a very simple background to something with rich texture and color. You can even put your subject in front of a totally different real-world background. The technique is the same for both. It lets you practice your selection skills and your use of layers. The possibilities are endless and can keep you up late at night trying them all out!

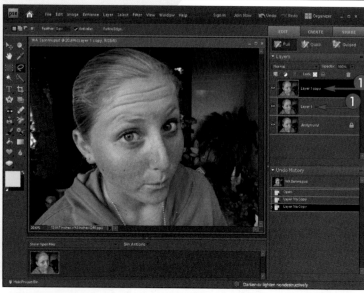

① Copy your photograph to two new layers by pressing Ctrl+J twice.

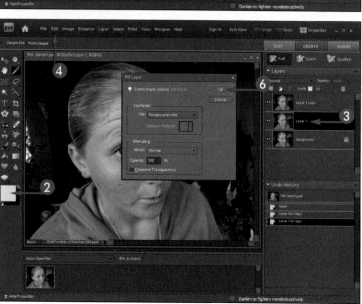

② Pick an interesting foreground color by clicking it and using the Foreground color dialog box.

③ Click the middle layer to make it active.

④ Click Edit and then select Fill Layer.

⑤ Click the Contents Use drop-down menu and select Foreground Color.

⑥ Click OK.

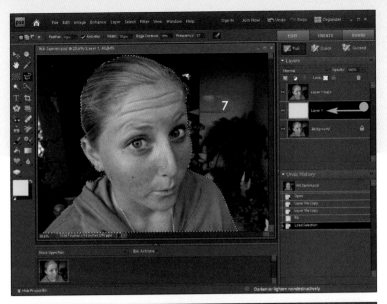

● The middle layer is now the same as your foreground color.

You cannot see this color in the actual picture because another layer, the same picture, is covering the second layer.

**DIFFICULTY LEVEL**

**7** Make a selection around your subject using whatever selection tools work best.

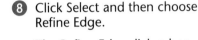

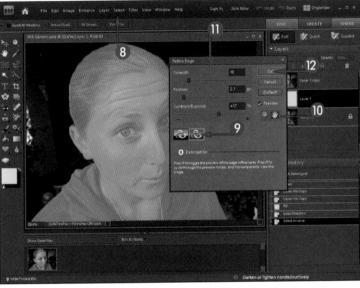

**8** Click Select and then choose Refine Edge.

The Refine Edge dialog box opens.

**9** Click the red icon to get an overlay that better displays the edge.

**10** Use the Zoom and Hand tools as needed to magnify the image and move it around so you can better see the edge.

**11** Adjust the Smooth, Feather, and Contract/Expand sliders to refine the edge of the selection.

**12** Click OK.

---

**TIPS**

### Important!

Watch those edges as you go around your subject. The selection edge really has a big impact on how well the background works with your subject. Select your subject using whatever selection tools work best for you and the subject. Add to and subtract from that selection using the Shift and Alt keys.

### Did You Know?

The red overlay that appears when you use the overlay button in Refine Edge helps you see changes in the selection edge. The red is where nothing is selected; you clearly see the selected area that has no red. This edge shows blending, feathering, and so on, which is not seen with the normal selection edge.

### Try This!

Once you start putting backgrounds behind your subject, be aware of sharpness. Normally you will want your subject to be sharp and the background to be less sharp. Because the background is new anyway, you can blur it as much as you want with Gaussian Blur. Usually you want to have at least a slight blur on that new background.

# ADD A NEW BACKGROUND
## for your subject

So what can you put as a new background for your subject? Bright colors work great with young people. Muted colors work well with gentle portraits. Textures give dimension to a background, and Photoshop Elements offers a lot of textures if you experiment with the filters in the Filter menu.

You can open a totally different photograph and use it for a background. An easy way to do this is to make a new layer in that photo using Ctrl+J, and then select the Move tool at the upper left of the toolbox. Click the layer and drag it to the photograph of your subject needing a new background. Be sure that your cursor has gone completely over the edges of the photograph and then release the mouse button. This picture is dropped onto your picture, over the active layer. Move it around with the Move tool, and then blur it so that it looks more natural.

⑬ Click the top layer to be sure it is active.

⑭ Press Delete or Backspace.

The selected area is removed from the top layer and the new background shows through.

⑮ If the edges need improvement, press Ctrl and then click the top layer.

This selects the subject.

⑯ Press Ctrl+Shift+I to invert the selection.

⑰ Click Select, choose Modify, and then choose Expand.

The Expand Selection dialog box opens.

⑱ Type a low number of pixels.

⑲ Click OK.

20 Click Select and choose Feather.

The Feather Selection dialog box opens.

# 67
## CONTINUED

21 Type a low number of pixels, the same or less than used for Expand Selection.

22 Click OK.

23 Click the Eraser tool.

24 Choose a brush size appropriate to the size of your edges.

25 Choose a soft-edged brush.

26 Press Ctrl+H to hide the selection edge.

27 Erase along the edge of your subject wherever there are problems.

The selection allows you to erase only along the edge.

## TIPS

### More Options!
Once you have dragged a real photograph onto your picture for a new background, you can also drag it below your subject if the new layer comes into the Layers palette on top. To resize this picture layer, go to the Image menu, and then choose Resize and Scale. You then simply drag the sides, top, bottom, and corners in and out as needed.

### Try This!
Freely experiment for backgrounds. You can discover all sorts of backgrounds by using different colors and different images, and then just trying a lot of filters in the Filter menu. You can even copy your original picture below your subject and apply filters to that layer just for the effect.

### Try This!
Look for backgrounds that complement your subject. Sure, you can put a subject against some wacky background, but if the light, contrast, and tonality of your subject do not really go with that background, the picture will never look right. It will look like the subject and background were just pasted against each other.

# Chapter 7

# Size and Sharpen Photos

Digital photos have to be sized for specific uses. They are not like using film. With film, you simply put the negative into an enlarger and make the picture bigger or smaller as needed — the original image never changes. You cannot do that with a digital photo. Once a picture is resized to a small image, for example, that resulting small image file cannot be resized with any quality to a big picture.

In general, do all of your processing work on a photograph using a master Photoshop or PSD file, and then save that master file for any future resizing purposes. The best way to do

this is to create a new file for every new size of picture that you need. You do not want to resize your master file and then save over that because you will not be able to get back to the original size from that saved file.

Some photographers resize an image for every small change in size that they need. This is rarely necessary. You will not find a lot of quality difference changing from an 8-x-10-inch photo to a 5-x-7-inch photo, for example. But you will see a difference if you try to use an 8-x-10-inch photo for a 2-x-3-inch wallet-size image or vice versa.

# Top 100

# BASIC WORKFLOW
## for image sizing

Photoshop Elements puts all sizing controls into one place: Image Size in the Image menu's Resize submenu. To use the image sizing options effectively, it helps to understand how Photoshop Elements structures the resizing of an image. You can make a picture bigger or smaller by either changing how many pixels are in a picture or by changing the spacing of the pixels in an image file.

The program uses some rather complex algorithms to make an image file bigger or smaller in pixels, yet retain the best possible quality for the picture. You have to tell Photoshop Elements how to handle your particular picture, which is what the options in Image Size are all about. The right choices are fairly straightforward; however, some options can cause you problems if you choose them inappropriately. This is not something to worry about, but you do need to pay attention to what you are doing.

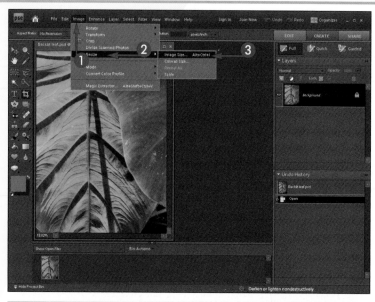

❶ Click Image.

❷ Select Resize.

❸ Choose Image Size.

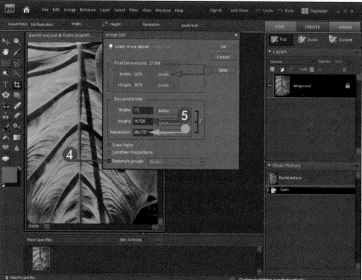

The Image Size dialog box opens.

❹ Be sure Resample Image is unchecked.

❺ Type any size in width or height and the other dimension is automatically chosen.

● Resolution changes because at this point you are only moving pixels closer together or farther apart.

● Pixel Dimensions do not change because there are no new pixels.

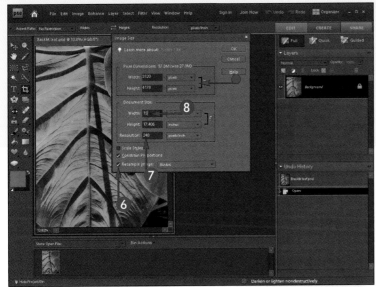

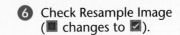

**6** Check Resample Image (■ changes to ☑).

This tells the program to add or subtract pixels to change an image size.

**7** Type a Resolution.

**8** Type a new width or height.

● Pixel Dimensions now change because new pixels will be created.

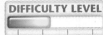

# 68

**DIFFICULTY LEVEL**

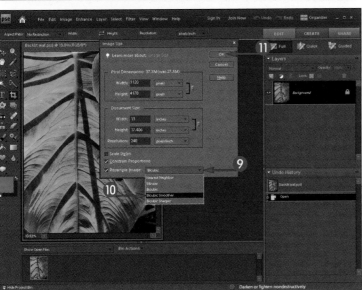

**9** Click the Resample Image drop-down menu.

**10** Choose Bicubic Smoother if your photograph will be enlarged, that is, Pixel Dimensions increase.

Choose Bicubic Sharper if your photograph will be reduced in size.

**11** Click OK to resize the picture.

---

**TIPS**

### Did You Know?

Image sizing is not designed to give you a specific size such as 8 x 10 inches or 11 x 14 inches. It is designed to make your overall picture larger or smaller. If you want a very specific size, then you need to use Image Size to get a correct height or width, and then use the Crop tool to get the final size.

### Caution!

Most photographers will always leave the Constrained Proportions box checked. This means that your picture will be resized according to the original proportions of the photograph. If this box is unchecked, you will get wildly distorted photographs from your resizing.

### Did You Know?

When you enlarge an image's size and pixels are created, the differences between those pixels must be smoothed out so your photo has maximum quality. That is why you use Bicubic Smoother. When you reduce the size of an image, detail is thrown out. To retain the sharpest detail, you use Bicubic Sharper.

# Size photos
# FOR PRINTING

Inkjet printers do a fantastic job in creating superb photo quality for your prints. But to get the optimum quality, the image file must be sized properly for a given print output size. You will not get the best results if you simply print any image size from one master file that has a specific size and resolution. In fact, you can get a decline in print image quality from both too little and too much resolution.

Resolution is a very important part of image sizing for a print. You need to create an image with a printing resolution. All inkjet printers create a high-quality print using resolutions between 200–360 ppi or pixels per inch. If you can resize your image without resampling the picture and stay within this range, you can use your master image file for printing. You do not need to make and save new copies of this image until you start resampling the picture.

① Click Image.

② Select Resize.

③ Choose Image Size.

The Image Size dialog box opens.

④ Be sure Resample Image is unchecked.

⑤ Type 200 for Resolution.

⑥ Note the width and height because this is the maximum size for printing without resampling.

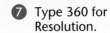

**7** Type 360 for Resolution.

**8** Note the width and height because this is the minimum size for printing without resampling.

You now know how big or small you can print without increasing or decreasing the number of pixels.

**9** Check Resample Image when you want to change the size of your picture beyond the range represented by 200–360 ppi (■ changes to ☑).

Use 200 ppi for bigger pictures and 360 ppi for smaller pictures.

**10** Choose Bicubic Smoother if your photograph will be enlarged, that is, Pixel Dimensions increase.

Choose Bicubic Sharper if your photograph will be reduced in size.

**11** Click OK to resize the picture.

---

### Important!

The resolution of an image is not the same thing as the resolution of a printer. *Image resolution* refers to the way pixels create tones and details in a photo. *Printer resolution* has to do with how the printer puts down ink droplets on the paper. They mean very different things.

### Did You Know?

*Pixels per inch*, or *ppi*, is a standard way of measuring the density of pixels in a picture, which is also a measure of resolution. Pixels alone are not enough information. To understand resolution, you must have pixels combined with inches, which is an indication of how many pixels fit in a linear dimension.

### Did You Know?

The type of paper used for printing affects the ppi needed in the original image. Matte finishes can handle lower resolutions quite nicely, whereas glossy papers tend to require higher resolutions. Do your own tests and see how resolution affects the look of an image on the papers that you use.

# Size photos
# FOR E-MAIL

Sharing photos via e-mail is a great way to get your pictures in front of friends, family, and others. You can, for example, take pictures of your kids playing soccer in the afternoon and then send off copies of those pictures to the grandparents that night. Even if the grandparents lived nearby, this was never possible with film.

A common problem with e-mail pictures, however, is that a lot of people simply download the pictures from the camera and send those image files attached to e-mail. That can be a real problem because the high-megapixel cameras of today have quite sizable files, even when using JPEG. This can cause problems for the recipient of the e-mail when the images take too long to download or even crash the recipient's e-mail software. You can totally avoid this problem by sizing your pictures properly for e-mail purposes.

1 Click Image.

2 Select Resize.

3 Choose Image Size.

The Image Size dialog box opens.

4 Check Resample Image (☐ changes to ☑).

5 Type **100** for Resolution.

6 Type **8** for the longest side, whether it is width or height.

This gives a good, small image file for standard e-mailing purposes.

**DIFFICULTY LEVEL**

⑦ Type **150** for Resolution.

⑧ Type **8** for the longest side, whether it is width or height.

This gives a small image file that can be both e-mailed and printed.

⑨ Click OK.

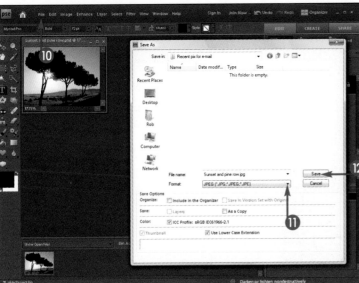

Your image now appears smaller in size in the Elements workspace.

***Note:*** *You can make it fill the workspace again by pressing Ctrl+0.*

⑩ Click File and choose Save As.

The Save As dialog box appears.

⑪ Choose JPEG for the file format.

⑫ Click Save.

The JPEG Quality dialog box appears.

⑬ Select a moderate JPEG Quality setting of 6–9 and then click OK.

---

**TIPS**

### Did You Know?

A resolution of 100 ppi is easy to remember and works fine for displaying pictures that have been sent by e-mail. Few monitors actually display at 72 ppi anymore, which used to be the recommended resolution for e-mail.

### Did You Know?

For optimum printing quality, you will generally choose a resolution of at least 200 ppi. However, 150 ppi gives an acceptable, photo-quality print, at the same time allowing you to have a significantly smaller image size for e-mailing.

### More Options!

When you save an image as a new JPEG file, you get a dialog box with options for JPEG saving. As you change the Quality setting, you see a number appear under the Preview check box. This number is the resulting size of your image at the Quality chosen. For e-mail, Quality numbers of 6–9 are common and work fine.

# SHARPEN PHOTOS
## with Unsharp Mask

You can only sharpen pixels in Photoshop Elements. This means that you must sharpen a flattened file saved for a specific purpose or use a technique that creates a pixel-based layer for sharpening.

Sharpening in Photoshop Elements is designed to get the optimum amount of sharpness from your original image based on a sharp picture to begin with. It does not help blurry or out-of-focus pictures.

For a variety of reasons, images coming from a digital sensor are not optimally sharp. Most cameras apply

some sharpening to a JPEG file as it is processed inside the camera. No sharpening is applied to a RAW file. Yet, no matter what image comes into Photoshop Elements, it usually needs some degree of sharpening. Unsharp Mask is a good tool for sharpening in Elements. The name comes from a traditional process used to sharpen photos for printing plates in the commercial printing industry. It is not about making unsharp pictures sharp.

**①** Click Enhance.

**②** Select Unsharp Mask.

The Unsharp Mask dialog box opens.

**③** Type 130–180 for Amount.

Amount is the intensity of the sharpening.

**④** Type 1.0–1.5 for Radius.

Radius affects how sharpness is enhanced around an edge.

**DIFFICULTY LEVEL**

**⑤** Type 3–6 for Threshold.

Threshold affects how small details such as noise are sharpened.

**⑥** Click OK.

---

## TIPS

### Caution!

Beware of over-sharpening. Although you can increase the Amount and Radius to make a blurry picture look sort of sharp or make sharpness look intense, this can also damage your photo in a lot of ways. It makes tonalities look harsh, and you lose fine tones and colors in the picture.

### More Options!

The preview window in the Unsharp Mask dialog box can be very helpful. Click a part of the whole picture to show detail in the preview. Click on and off the preview picture itself to see how sharpening is being applied. Click the preview picture and drag to move its position around.

### More Options!

Change your sharpening based on the subject. Landscapes and architecture typically do well with a higher sharpening Amount and Radius. People photography, especially close-ups of faces, usually need less sharpening, even going as low as 100 for Amount and under 1 for Radius.

# SHARPEN PHOTOS
## with Adjust Sharpness

Adjust Sharpness is a more recent addition to Photoshop Elements for sharpening as compared to Unsharp Mask. It uses advanced algorithms for sharpening to get the maximum detail possible from a photograph. You might wonder why not just use this way of sharpening all the time. The reason is because of noise and Threshold.

Adjust Sharpness does not have a Threshold control. This means that if you have noise in your picture, the noise is likely to be sharpened just as much as anything else in the picture. The result is that the noise becomes more visible. It certainly does not hurt to try Adjust Sharpness. If noise shows up too much from that, then go back to Unsharp Mask.

Adjust Sharpness also works very well for highly detailed pictures, such as landscapes and architecture. But when you need more gentle sharpening, such as with people, you may find that Unsharp Mask works better.

1 Click Enhance.

2 Select Adjust Sharpness.

The Adjust Sharpness dialog box opens.

3 Check More Refined (■ changes to ☑).

4 Click and drag in the preview window until you find a good place to check sharpness.

Alternately, click your cursor on something that should be sharp in the photo itself.

⑤ Type 100–160 for Amount.

Amount is slightly different from Amount in Unsharp Mask.

# #72

⑥ Type 1.0–1.5 for Radius.

Radius is also slightly different from Radius in Unsharp Mask.

⑦ Click OK.

---

**TIPS**

### Important!

Because noise can become more obvious in Adjust Sharpness, it is important that you look for it. Enlarge the picture in the Preview box with the plus button underneath the image. Check areas like dark parts of an image that have been brightened and the sky. These areas usually show noise faster than any other areas.

### More Options!

Click Remove in Adjust Sharpness and a drop-down menu appears that tells Adjust Sharpness how to deal with sharpening. You can sometimes better sharpen pictures that have motion blur by selecting Motion Blur. And sometimes you can get sharper pictures when the subject is slightly out of focus by selecting Lens Blur.

### More Options!

If you read anything about Photoshop and Photoshop Elements, you will find a variety of formulas for Unsharp Mask and Adjust Sharpness. Generally, these all work and can be worth a try. Every photographer uses different formulas because sharpness really does depend on the subject and on the personal tastes of the photographer.

# Sharpen photos
# WHEN YOU HAVE LAYERS

The sharpening features of Photoshop Elements must have pixels to work on. This presents a challenge when you work with layers. First, you need to have pixels in a layer in order to sharpen it; second, even if you do have pixels in a layer, you can sharpen only one layer at a time. Once you have finished working on a photograph using layers, you normally sharpen the whole picture, including everything that adjustment layers might do to it.

You do this by creating a special layer on top of all your other layers that merges those layers together into one pixel layer. You then sharpen that layer. Label it the sharpened layer so you know what it is. You can later go back and readjust anything underneath that layer, although you must create a new sharpened layer if you do.

① Click the top layer.

② Press Alt+Ctrl+Shift+E.

  You are pressing the modifier keys plus E.

● A new layer formed from a copy of the merged layers appears at the top of the layer stack.

③ Rename the layer *Sharpened Layer*.

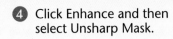

④ Click Enhance and then select Unsharp Mask.

The Unsharp Mask the dialog box opens.

⑤ Type 130–180 for Amount.

⑥ Type 1.0–1.5 for Radius.

⑦ Type 3–6 for Threshold.

⑧ Click OK.

**# 73**

**DIFFICULTY LEVEL**

● The sharpened layer is now sharpened, but nothing else in the photo is sharpened.

**TIPS**

### Did You Know?

Unsharp Mask can be very useful when sharpening the merged-layers layer in a many-layered file. When a lot of adjustment layers are applied to a photograph, especially a JPEG picture, you find noise and other image artifacts beginning to appear. These can be minimized by the use of a Threshold setting, which does not exist in Adjust Sharpness.

### Did You Know?

The Merge and Make New Layer command, Alt+Ctrl+Shift+E, is a fairly well-known command in the Photoshop world. However, it does not show up in any menus. You have to know of its existence and what it does in order to use it. This command is the same in both Photoshop and Photoshop Elements.

### Caution!

You need to be very careful that you click the top layer before using the Merge and Make New Layer command. This command places a layer anywhere in your layer stack, simply above whatever layer is active. This can get to be very confusing.

# SELECTIVELY SHARPEN
## parts of your photo

If you have a photograph with a close-up of a flower, and that flower is sharp whereas the background is out of focus, you really only need to sharpen the flower. If you have photographed a portrait with an out-of-focus background, the face needs to be sharp, but not the background.

In fact, you may not want to try sharpening out-of-focus areas at all for several reasons. A big reason is noise. Noise tends to show up more in autofocus

areas and does not need to be sharpened. Another reason is that odd little details can be sharpened in the out-of-focus area, degrading the visual quality of such a background. By restricting your sharpness to only the areas that need to be sharp, you will not have these problems. This technique is only for pictures with a distinct difference in sharpness between the subject and the rest of the image.

① Press Ctrl+J to duplicate your photo to a new layer.

Alternately, click the top layer of a layered file and press Alt+Ctrl+Shift+E.

② Click Enhance and then select Unsharp Mask.

The Unsharp Mask dialog box opens.

③ Type 130–180 for Amount.

④ Type 1.0–1.5 for Radius.

⑤ Type 3–8 for Threshold.

⑥ Click OK.

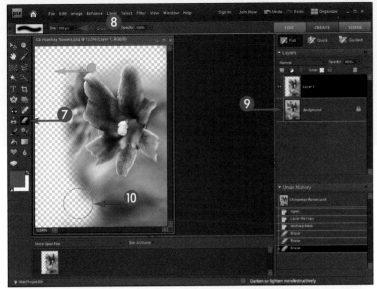

7 Click the Eraser tool in the toolbox.

8 Use a large, soft-edged brush to start.

9 Click the eye icon for the bottom layer, Background, to turn it off.

10 Begin to erase the unsharp parts of the picture.

● By turning off the bottom layer, you can more easily see what you are erasing.

Change your brush size as needed to go around your sharp subject and press Ctrl+Z to undo any mistakes.

11 Click the eye icon for the bottom layer, Background, to turn it back on.

The top layer is now a sharpened layer, but only where the original picture was sharp.

---

**TIPS**

### Caution!

Be wary of using high Threshold numbers. Threshold is very useful in minimizing the impact of sharpening on noise and other image detail problems called *artifacts*. But it can also affect small important detail as well. Keep Threshold under 6 when you can, but go up to a maximum of 12.

### Did You Know?

Sharpening is typically done at the end or at least toward the end of your image processing. The reason for this is that sharpening affects things like noise and other details. Such details will often be changed as you process the image. Sharpening too early can then mean that these details can be adversely affected as you work the image, causing problems with them.

### Attention!

Think about your subject as you sharpen your photograph. Sharpening is not a one-size-fits-all type of adjustment. Some subjects look great with high sharpness, such as a rocky landscape. Others, such as a person's face, look better with lower amounts of sharpness.

# Chapter 8

# Go Beyond the Basics

Once you have mastered the basics of working on images, you may want to look for other things to do with your pictures. One option is to convert your pictures to black-and-white. It was not all that long ago that color was the special type of photography and black-and-white was rather ordinary. At that time, black-and-white was commonly seen in every publication. Today, color is the most common way that pictures are seen. Black-and-white has become a very special way of dealing with pictures, giving images a unique look because they contrast with the very common color photos. Plus, black-and-white offers some really special ways of dealing with a subject.

Another fun thing that you can do with digital photography and Photoshop Elements is to create a panoramic photograph. These pictures are created from a series of images. The width or height of the scene is too great for your lens to include, so you make up for it by taking pictures across that scene. Alternately, you may like the format of a panoramic image, but you want a bigger photograph than is possible from simply cropping that format out of a single image. Photoshop Elements supports the multi-image panoramic quite well.

# Top 100

# Convert color photos to
# BLACK-AND-WHITE

With many digital cameras, you can set the camera to take a black-and-white photograph. The advantage to this is that you can see exactly what you get from a scene turned into black-and-white. The disadvantage is that the black-and-white image is locked into a JPEG file and cannot be changed.

Any black-and-white photo is created by changing the colors of the world into tones of black-and-white. When you convert a color image to black-and-white in Photoshop Elements, you have a lot of control as to

how to change the colors into tones of black-and-white. Controlling how you change colors into those tones can be an extremely important way to work because sometimes colors that stand out in a color image blend together when converted to black-and-white. Having the ability to change how this conversion occurs in the computer gives you much more power and flexibility in working with black-and-white.

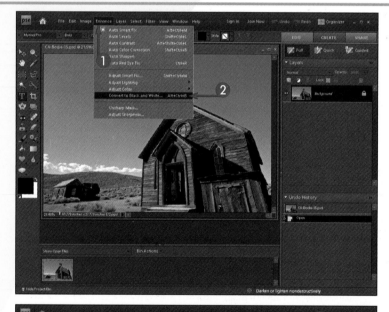

*Note: Do your normal processing of the color image first.*

**1** Click Enhance.

**2** Select Convert to Black and White.

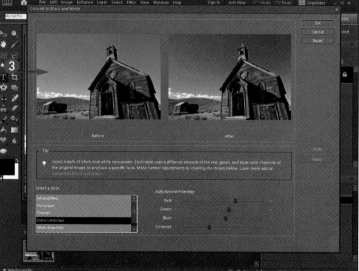

The Convert to Black and White dialog box opens.

**3** Compare the color and black-and-white images to see if you like the interpretation of the scene.

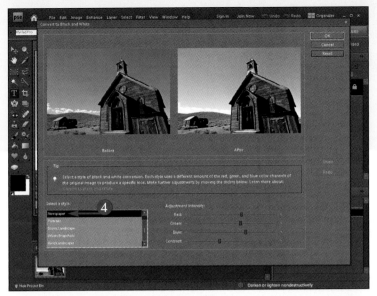

**4** Click different styles, or interpretations, of conversion and see how they work with your photo.

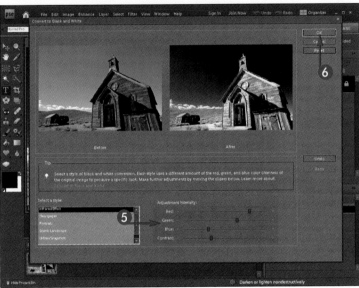

**5** Modify a style by changing the brightness of tones by adjusting the intensity of colors.

**6** Click OK.

## TIPS

### Important!
The default Photoshop Elements black-and-white conversion of your image should be seen purely as a starting point. Sometimes it looks fine, but most of the time you need to at least adjust the color sliders to refine how colors are changed into tones of gray.

### Did You Know?
Strong adjustments to a picture as it is converted to a black-and-white image can cause some undesirable effects. Watch out for noise appearing in areas that have had an extreme change. Also beware of breaks in the tonality, which will look like steps of tones, in smooth-toned areas such as skies.

### Did You Know?
RAW files always come into Camera Raw in Photoshop Elements as color images even if they were shot as black-and-white in the camera. One advantage to RAW for black-and-white is being able to use a 16-bit file. This allows for stronger tonal adjustments without breaks in smooth-toned areas.

# Adjust your photos in
# BLACK-AND-WHITE

The tonalities and gradations of grays are what give a black-and-white image its life. Because of that, these tonalities are very important. The first way that you get these tones and gradations is when you make the conversion from color to black-and-white. Sometimes your picture will look great at this point.

Often, however, you need to do more, using the same controls that are discussed in the rest of this book. Because a good strong black is very important to a good-looking black-and-white image, it can be very

helpful to reexamine the blacks in your photograph. You may want to set them to a higher point within the range of dark grays for a dramatic effect. Midtones are also very important, so you may want to reexamine them by the use of Color Curves. All black-and-white images are interpretations of the world because we do not see the world that way. Your interpretation is important and is affected by these adjustments.

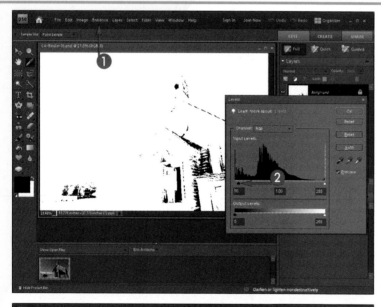

① Click Enhance, select Adjust Lighting, and then choose Levels.

② Press the Alt key as you move the black slider toward the right until you like the looks of your blacks.

   *Note: This can also be done using a Levels adjustment layer as discussed in task #45.*

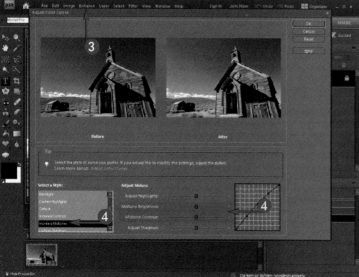

③ Click Enhance, select Adjust Color, and then choose Adjust Color Curves.

④ Adjust the midtones until you like the overall brightness of the picture and how the tonalities look.

⑤ Examine your photo for tonal imbalances or areas that should be darker.

⑥ Click the Adjustment Layer icon and choose Brightness/Contrast.

⑦ Adjust Brightness to darken the picture.

# 76

DIFFICULTY LEVEL

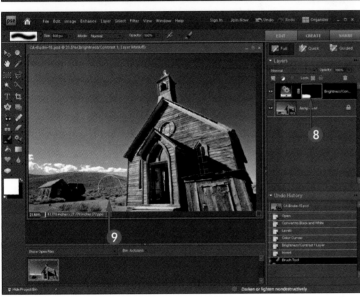

⑧ Press Ctrl+I to invert the layer mask to black and block the darkening effect.

⑨ Use a soft white paintbrush to brush in the darkening where needed in the picture.

## TIPS

### Important!

Grayscale and Remove Color are two additional black-and-white adjustments in Photoshop Elements. They are not recommended for most black-and-white conversion because they change color to black-and-white tones in one and only one way. You have no ability to change this.

### Did You Know?

You will sometimes hear black-and-white images called grayscale. *Grayscale* is a term that simply refers to the way an image deals with color, in this case a scale of gray tones. The term tends to be used more by computer people than photographers.

### Did You Know?

Another term for black-and-white is *monochrome*. This tends to be a somewhat trendy way that some photographers talk about black-and-white, perhaps trying to sound cool as well. Monochrome actually refers to any image based on one color. This is not limited to gray and can include red, blue, or any other color.

# Create
# TONED IMAGES

One of the classic ways that photographers worked with black-and-white images was to tone them. This meant adding a slight color to the black-and-white image. The most common was a warm tone called sepia tone. Another common toning color was a slight blue for a cool effect.

This can be an effective way to enrich your black-and-white images. You have a whole range of possibilities here, from a very subtle effect that provides just a

hint of color to strongly colored effects for special purposes. One advantage of a toned image as compared to a pure black-and-white photo is that it usually prints very nicely on any inkjet printer.

Photographers sometimes create dramatic posters by using a strongly colored black-and-white image. For that sort of effect, they often create rather dramatic black areas and white areas in the photograph that go beyond the simple black-and-white conversion.

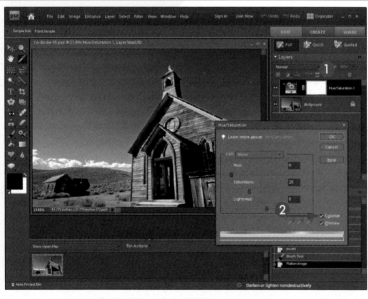

**①** Click the Adjustment Layer icon and choose Hue/Saturation.

**②** Click the Colorize check box (■ changes to ☑).

The image now has a color and is a monochrome image based on that color.

**③** For a sepia-toned image, use a 35–50 amount for Hue to get a warm tone.

**④** For a cool-toned image, use 180–210 points for Hue.

**⑤** Change Saturation lower for a less intense color or higher for a more intense color.

**⑥** Use the layer Opacity to change the intensity of the color as needed.

---

# 77

## TIPS

### More Options!

As you make a color image into a black-and-white photo, you may find it helpful to save different versions of your pictures. An easy way to do this is to simply use Duplicate in the File menu. This creates an immediate copy with a new name and saves it to the same folder as your original. Now do the changes to the copy.

### Try This!

The toning effect can be modified by the use of layer blending modes. Click the blending modes drop-down menu, which says Normal to start, and then try the blending modes grouped under Overlay. Some of these get pretty extreme, but all of them can create interesting effects with your photograph.

### More Options!

Have fun with toning colors. There is no right or wrong except what you like or dislike. Although most black-and-white photographs probably do not look their best with extreme colors, it can be fun to try unexpected colors to create unique images that gain attention for special purposes.

# Use the Smart Brush
# FOR CREATIVE EFFECTS

A fun special effect is to adjust part of your picture one way and another area completely different. A good example of this is a photograph in which the entire subject is in color, but the background is black-and-white. Another example could include only a very small part of the picture having color, such as a young girl holding a red rose and only the rose is in color.

You can do special effects like this with layers by copying a photo to a layer, applying a unique effect to

the top layer, and then erasing from that layer wherever you want to reveal the original image underneath. You can also paint such effects literally onto your picture by using the Smart Brush. The Smart Brush adds an adjustment layer to your photograph and then uses the Quick Selection tool with the layer mask to smartly apply the adjustment where you brush.

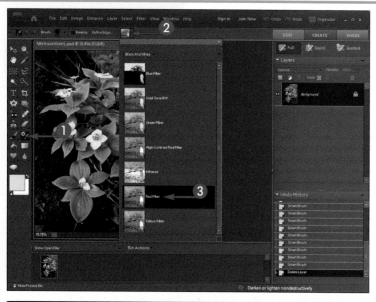

① Click the Smart Brush in the toolbox.

② Click the Smart Brush effects icon.

③ Choose the effect you want to paint on your picture.

④ Select an appropriate brush size for your photograph.

⑤ Begin painting on the part of the picture where you want the effect to occur.

● A special adjustment layer is added to your photograph.

Photoshop Elements smartly finds similar areas to use for your effect.

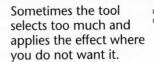

## 78

DIFFICULTY LEVEL

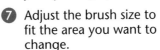

Sometimes the tool selects too much and applies the effect where you do not want it.

6 Change the effect brush to an effect removal brush by clicking the small brush icon with the minus sign at the upper left corner of your photograph.

7 Adjust the brush size to fit the area you want to change.

8 Click that area.

It often works better to click areas to remove an effect and then brush over the area.

9 Press Ctrl+H to hide the selection edge so that you can better see what is happening to your picture.

Revise the effect as needed.

10 Click Refine Edge to feather and smooth the edge so that the effect blends naturally.

TIPS

### Important!

Unless your background is very simple, you will find that you must change brush sizes as you use the Smart Brush. A large brush works fine to start, but then it captures too much of a photograph. At that point you need a smaller brush. Remember to use the [ and ] keys to quickly change your brush size.

### Try This!

Because everything done with a Smart Brush is done with an adjustment layer plus layer mask, nothing is done permanently to your picture. This means you can freely experiment with the Smart Brush effects. If you really do not like something, simply delete the layer by dragging it to the trash can icon.

### More Options!

The Smart Brush offers a lot of interesting adjustments that you can apply to your picture. They all work the same way in that an effect is applied to your picture in specific areas as you paint over the image. Explore the complete list of Smart Brush choices and you will find a number of them that will probably work with your types of pictures.

# Create a
# HAND-COLORED LOOK

A classic effect for black-and-white photography was made by painting colors by hand onto a black-and-white print. Most of this was done in a very realistic way, but some of this hand coloring was done in quite unusual ways as well. Either way, it required a bit of effort to do because you had to have prints made and the right paint for working on the images. If you made a mistake, you had to throw out the print and start all over again.

You can create exactly this effect in Photoshop Elements, yet you do not have to worry about making mistakes, nor do you need any special paints. In addition, you have a great deal of flexibility over the colors you use, and you can change any of them whenever you want. This can be a fun way of creating a striking new look for your photographs.

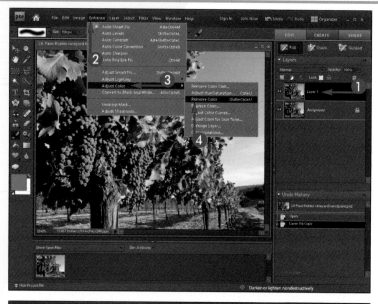

1 Duplicate your photo by pressing Ctrl+J.

2 Click Enhance.

3 Choose Adjust Color.

4 Choose Remove Color.

You now have a black-and-white image on top of a color photo.

5 Click the New Layer icon to add a blank layer.

6 Name that layer based on a color you want to use for the photo.

7 Repeat to add as many layers as you think you will need based on colors you plan to use.

8 Click the eye icon for the black-and-white layer to turn it off.

9 Click the Eyedropper in the toolbox.

10 Click a color in the picture you want to use.

● This color now appears as the foreground color.

## 79

DIFFICULTY LEVEL

11 Click the eye icon for the black-and-white layer to turn it back on.

12 Click the layer you want to use for this color.

13 Click the Paintbrush.

14 Choose a good-sized, soft-edged brush.

15 Select Color for the layer blending mode.

16 Paint over the photo where you want this color.

---

## TIPS

### Did You Know?

You may wonder if it is better to create the black-and-white layer using Remove Color or by making your own black-and-white adjustment. This really depends on personal taste and individual photographs. There is no right or wrong way to do this.

### Try This!

A quick-and-easy way to get to the Eyedropper when you are using any other tool is to simply press the Alt key. This immediately changes whatever cursor you are using to the Eyedropper. You can then click a color and it will appear in the foreground color; release the Alt key and the original tool returns.

### More Options!

Do not worry if you do not have the right number of layers when you get started on this technique. The only reason for adding layers at the beginning is to get you started with a set of layers that will separate your colors. You can add or subtract layers later if your plans change as you work on the image.

# Create a
# HAND-COLORED LOOK

The hand-colored or hand-painted look really has a lot of possibilities for the photographer. There is no one way of using this technique. You can choose realistic colors or you can decide to color your subject and its surroundings in some totally new way. You can make this effect look very pale and pastel by both the choice of your colors and the Opacity of the layer. You can also make this effect look very intense by choosing very saturated colors and keeping the layers at 100% Opacity.

You also do not have to color the entire photograph. Sometimes it can be very interesting to only add one or just a few colors into a picture. You can also be as precise in your coloring as you want, but many photographers find that the effect looks quite interesting if edges are not precise.

⓱ Click the next layer.

⓲ Click the foreground color.

The Select foreground color dialog box appears.

⓳ Click a color you want to use.

⓴ Click OK.

The foreground color changes to the selected color.

㉑ Paint on the new color.

● Be sure the layer blending mode is set to Color.

**㉒** Change the Opacity of the layer until the color looks right.

● Continue this process, layer by layer, until you have finished painting color on your image.

### Try This!
You can get the colors used for painting from two places, as you have seen in this task: from the original picture or from a foreground color. Try both techniques to see which one gives you the colors that best suit your needs and your photograph.

### Important!
In this technique, you have been using a separate color layer for each color. It is possible to put more than one color on a layer, but this is not recommended. You are more likely to have problems in adjusting colors if you have more than one color on a layer. Keep them separate and you will find that your image work has more flexibility, too.

### More Options!
As you paint a color onto your photograph, change the brush size as you go to better match changes within the photograph. In addition, use the Eraser at different sizes to remove areas of color that have spilled onto places where you do not want that color.

# Photograph a scene
# FOR A PANORAMIC IMAGE

Digital photography has meant a real increase in the popularity of a panoramic image. The panoramic image is like a wide-screen movie: it is physically a very wide photo compared to its height. Although you can crop a photograph to get a panoramic look to an image, the problem is that your picture can never be very big because it is limited by the maximum size of the image file.

A multi-image panoramic photo is created by shooting two or more images across a scene and then merging those together in the computer. This type of panoramic shot gives you a very large image because your original image file is actually quite a bit smaller than the final photo. This means you can make very large prints without any loss in quality. In addition, you can shoot a wider view of the scene than is possible otherwise, including a full 360° photograph.

Begin your panoramic photo by finding a scene that has distinctive photo elements from the left to right.

1 Find a beginning.

2 Include an interesting middle.

3 Finish with an end.

Next, set up your tripod.

4 Level the top of the tripod, below the tripod head.

5 Level the camera.

**6** Set your camera to Manual exposure.

Set one exposure for the scene to be used for all images.

**7** Shoot a series of pictures across the scene.

**8** Overlap the pictures by 30–50% so that they can blend well in Photoshop Elements.

---

**TIPS**

### Try This!

You can do verticals in a panoramic format as well. This becomes a tall, narrow image. The process is the same except that you shoot a series of images that overlap going up and down, rather than left to right. This can be a great way to photograph a waterfall, for example.

### Important!

Manual exposure is very important when you are shooting panoramic images. If you shoot your camera on automatic, you will get variations of exposure among the series of photos you take across the scene. That variation of exposure makes them much more difficult to blend together.

### More Options!

You can level your tripod and camera in several ways. A simple, compact level from the hardware store can help get you started. You can also get a level that fits into your camera's flash hot shoe that will help you level the camera.

# MERGE PHOTOS
## for a panoramic picture

Now that you have your photos shot, you are ready to merge them in Photoshop Elements. Photoshop Elements has a very powerful merge feature called Photomerge. This feature includes a number of possibilities on how you can work with your panoramic images.

However, the basics are very simple. You tell Photoshop Elements what pictures to work with. Photoshop Elements examines those pictures, comparing the areas where they overlap and then

aligning the images. This is why it is so important to give a good overlap to your photographs as you are taking the pictures — the program lines up the images one to the next so that these overlapped areas match. Similarly, this is why it is important to level your camera; otherwise, the matched individual pictures will line up with each other in a very crooked way. Finally, Photoshop Elements puts these pictures together as a panoramic image.

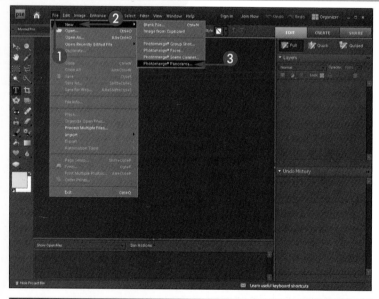

1. Click File.
2. Select New.
3. Choose Photomerge Panorama.

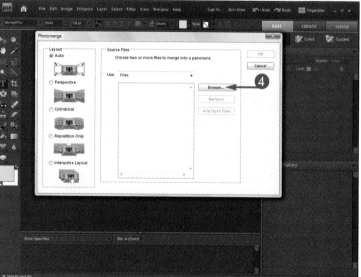

The Photomerge dialog box opens.

4. Click Browse.

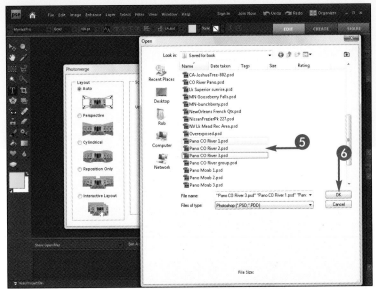

The Open dialog box opens.

**⑤** Select the series of images that make up your panorama.

Click the first one and then Shift+click the last one to select the others in between.

**⑥** Click OK.

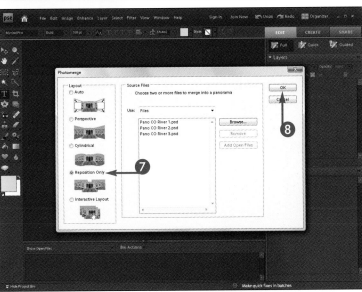

**⑦** Under Layout, click Reposition Only ( ⊙ changes to ⊙ ).

**⑧** Click OK.

### Try This!
Sometimes you will find that individual pieces of your panoramic image do not blend together as well as you would like. Because Photoshop Elements puts the individual pictures for a panorama into layers, you have a good opportunity for adjusting individual pictures to make them better match the rest. Simply select that area and work on the picture directly on that layer.

### Try This!
When is the best time to process individual panoramic images? Before putting them into the panorama or after? There is no simple answer to this. Sometimes working on individual pictures before combining them is easier. Other times it is better to work with them in the layers because this gives you a lot of flexibility.

### More Options!
When you open Photomerge, you notice that you have a choice with the Use box of either folders or files. Some photographers merge together a lot of images into one. To keep track of all those images, they often find it easier to put each panorama group into its own folder. This way they can go right to the folder when in Photomerge.

# MERGE PHOTOS
## for a panoramic picture

Photoshop Elements does most of the work for a panorama for you. The program does offer you several different options for how to put together your panoramic image. A common look for a panorama is to use the Reposition Only option. This simply lines up the pictures where they overlap and blends them together in a very straightforward manner.

Perspective puts the pictures together with a perspective effect that makes the image look like a bow tie. If you are photographing inside something so that parts of your picture are in front and directly to the sides of you, this option may help line things up better. Cylindrical maps the image onto imaginary cylinders, which sometimes helps things line up better and lines go together in really wide panoramic shots. Interactive layout requires you to do a little more work in lining up the individual images that make up your panoramic shot.

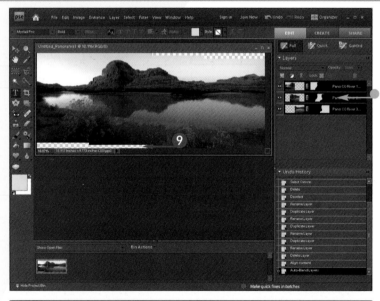

A panoramic image is created based on your group of photos.

- Each of the photos is placed into a layer with automatic layer masks to help blend it with the others.

**9** Look over your photo to check where the overlap occurs between pictures to see if there are problems that need to be fixed.

**10** Click the layer mask of a layer that has blending challenges.

**11** Click the Paintbrush.

**12** Select white for the foreground color.

**13** Paint over edge areas that need better blending.

Use both white and black colors for the layer mask as needed.

**14** Click the Crop tool.

**15** Click and drag your cursor to create a crop box over the image.

**16** Press Enter or click the green check mark.

# 81 CONTINUED

**17** Click the New Layer icon to add an empty layer over the panoramic.

**18** Click the Clone Stamp tool in the toolbox.

**19** Check All Layers in the options toolbar (■ changes to ☑).

**20** Select a reasonable brush size to deal with the edge gap on a panoramic image.

Press Alt and click once to set a clone-from point near the problem area.

**21** Clone over the gap.

## TIPS

### Try This!

Sometimes it is hard to see the edges where your pictures overlap in the Photomerged output. Clicking layers on and off so you can see the edges better helps a lot. You will often find both problems and opportunities for your image when you do this.

### Important!

When your panoramic image is basically complete, you can continue to adjust tonalities and colors. At this point, however, you should adjust them with adjustment layers. An adjustment layer above the top photo in your panoramic image now adjusts the entire panorama. You can limit adjustments to certain layers by the use of the layer mask.

### More Options!

If your photos really need a bit of work, it can be best to open the individual files first into Photoshop Elements. There you can adjust the pictures and compare each one as you go so that they do match when they go into the panorama. Then, when Photomerge is opened, simply click the Add Open Files button.

# Software Plug-Ins Make Work Easier

Plug-ins are specialized software programs that "plug into" a larger host program. They offer new features that make the original program more effective or that the host program does not have at all. Nearly all plug-ins that work with Photoshop also work with Photoshop Elements.

One of the big benefits of using a plug-in within Photoshop Elements is that it can expand your efficiency and the power of the program. Many photographers discover that with the use of a few plug-ins, they can easily equal work that more sophisticated photographers do with Photoshop. And they can do this at a fraction of the cost of buying Photoshop!

In this chapter you will find a variety of plug-ins offering a whole range of features for Photoshop Elements users. Few photographers will need or even want all of them. The purpose of this chapter is to give you an idea of what is possible from using plug-ins. They do add to the cost of working on images on the computer, but better efficiency and new imaging possibilities can make that cost worthwhile. You can always try any of these out by downloading trial versions from the manufacturers' Web sites. This way you can make a decision at no cost as to how valuable they might be for you.

# Top 100

# USE COLOR EFEX
## for quick creative adjustments

Nik Software is a company that specializes in plug-ins for photographers. Many plug-ins for Photoshop are really geared more toward designers and special effects than for the average photographer's use. Nik Software creates plug-ins that really seem to speak to photographers' needs.

Color Efex is a plug-in with a whole range of ways of adjusting your photograph. These include very direct effects such as changing the brightness balance of certain colors, adding a graduated neutral density filter effect, and getting more richness from foliage.

They also include adjustments that can fix problems in the picture such as a dynamic skin softener, a skylight filter, and a white neutralizer. Very creative effects are included such as mimicking the look of infrared film, creating a glamour glow look, and making a pastel image from your original. All of these are in an interface that allows you to see the effects directly, plus you can control how the effects are applied to the picture.

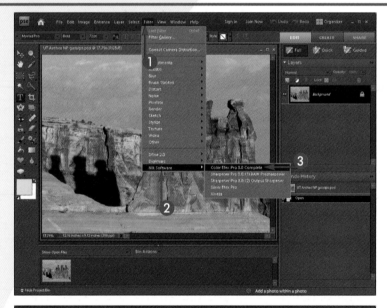

*Note: Plug-ins must be installed before they show up in Photoshop Elements.*

**1** Click Filter.

**2** Select Nik Software.

**3** Choose Color Efex.

The Color Efex plug-in interface appears.

**4** Choose an effect from the left side.

● The effect appears in the center window.

**5** Control the effect with the sliders at the upper right.

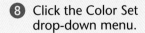

**8** Click the Color Set drop-down menu.

A drop-down menu of colors for the effect appears.

You can run your cursor across the colors to see the effects on the photograph.

**9** Choose a color that works with your subject.

**10** Click the Control Points minus button.

**11** Click a part of the photo where you want to reduce the effect, such as to remove the color from clouds.

**12** Use the sliders associated with the control point to adjust this change.

**13** Click OK.

## TIPS

### Important!

Do your basic image processing before you use a plug-in. You want to be sure that your blacks are set properly, the midtones look good, and colors are corrected before you start making major changes to the photograph. You must start with a good photograph before using the processing power of a plug-in.

### Did You Know?

Color Efex provides three different graduated filter effects. Graduated Filters gives you a choice of colors for the effect. Graduated Neutral Density is for purely darkening part of the picture. Graduated User Defined allows you to pick your own colors for the effect. The special effects filter Graduated Fog applies a fog look.

### Check It Out!

You can learn more about Color Efex and other software plug-ins from Nik Software by going to their Web site, www.niksoftware.com. There you will find trial versions to download as well as a complete listing of all the features in their programs. Plus you will see some great examples of how the software can be put to work.

# SHARPEN EFFECTIVELY
## with Sharpener Pro

Sharpening in Photoshop Elements really is pretty straightforward. You can do all of your sharpening there without ever buying a plug-in. However, Nik Software Sharpener Pro does offer some unique sharpening features not available in Photoshop Elements. Sharpener Pro includes more-advanced sharpening algorithms than those in Photoshop Elements. In addition, this program lets you sharpen for very specific output, such as a print on a particular paper surface.

One very interesting part of this plug-in is its ability to control what exactly is sharpened. One problem with any sharpening is that it can sharpen noise in inappropriate ways. Sharpener Pro allows you to control sharpening both by using control points and by telling the program how much to sharpen areas based on colors in the actual photograph. For example, skies often have more noise than other areas, so it helps to eliminate sharpening from sky color.

*Note:* To begin, click Filter, select Nik Software, and choose Sharpener Pro 3 Output Sharpener. Sharpener Pro appears.

1️⃣ Click the drop-down menu below Output Sharpening.

2️⃣ Select the type of sharpening needed from the drop-down menu.

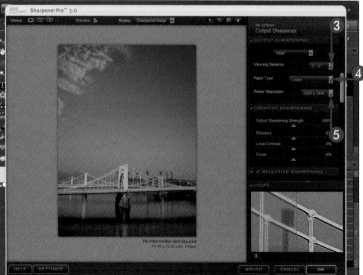

The Output Sharpening sliders change depending on the type of sharpening selected.

3️⃣ Choose a viewing distance.

4️⃣ Select a paper type based on the paper that you plan to use for printing.

5️⃣ Choose a printer resolution based on your printer.

**6** Leave Creative Sharpening at its defaults as you start using this plug-in.

● Be sure Selective Sharpening is checked.

**7** Click the drop-down menu below Selective Sharpening.

**8** Select Color Ranges.

**9** Click the pushpin icon under the Loupe preview.

**10** Click an important detail in the photograph to lock the Loupe view.

**11** Click an eyedropper next to a color.

**12** Click a color in the photograph that you want to affect.

**13** Adjust the slider to change how much sharpening is done related to that color.

**14** Repeat for other important colors.

**15** Click OK.

## TIPS

### Did You Know?
Sharpener Pro offers five different types of output sharpening: Display is for images displayed on a monitor, Inkjet is for images printed within an inkjet printer, Continuous Tone is for prints from photographic processes, Halftone is for commercial printing, and Hybrid Device is for special printers.

### More Options!
As you use sliders to make adjustments in Sharpener Pro or other Nik Software plug-ins, you can quickly reset them by double-clicking the slider itself. This can be very helpful when you are trying out adjustments and discover that a particular adjustment is getting confusing. This lets you reset it quickly.

### Did You Know?
The Loupe at the bottom right of Nik Software plug-ins is very useful in giving you information about details in your photograph. It displays a before and after image as you move your cursor across the picture. It also locks in a particular location when you click the pushpin icon and then click in the picture.

# REMOVE NOISE
## with Dfine

Noise can be a problem with digital photos. Sometimes noise shows up because of an underexposed image brightened to normal levels in Photoshop Elements. Other times it shows up when you need to use a high ISO setting on your camera because of low light levels or when you need a fast shutter speed. Although Photoshop Elements does have some very basic noise reduction controls, they really do not work very well when you have the challenge of strong noise in a picture.

For optimum noise reduction, you really need a dedicated noise reduction software program. Nik Software Dfine is a plug-in that works to control noise without hurting other detail in the photograph. Similar to Sharpener Pro, Dfine allows you to specifically define areas based on color to determine how much noise reduction you do. This gives you more control over how details are affected.

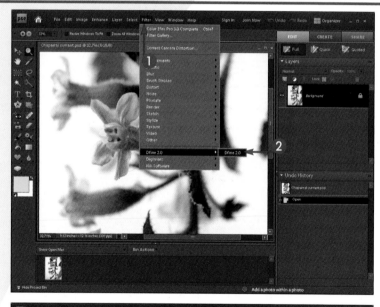

1 Click Filter.

2 Select Dfine 2.0.

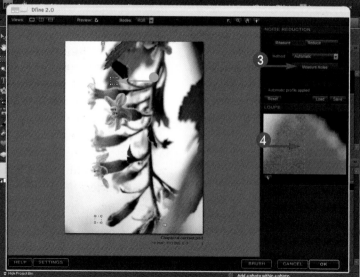

Dfine appears.

3 Click Measure Noise.

● Noise is measured at specific areas and reduced.

4 Move your cursor over the image to check the Loupe to see what noise reduction has occurred.

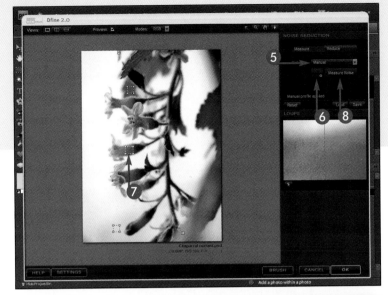

**⑤** Click the Method drop-down menu if more noise reduction is needed and select Manual.

**⑥** Click the Add Rectangle button below Manual.

**⑦** Draw a rectangle over an area with a noise problem.

**⑧** Click Measure Noise.

**DIFFICULTY LEVEL**

**⑨** Click Reduce.

**⑩** Click the Method drop-down menu and select Color Ranges.

**⑪** Click an eyedropper next to a color.

**⑫** Click a color in the photograph that you want to affect.

**⑬** Adjust the slider to change how much noise reduction is done related to that color.

**⑭** Repeat for other important colors.

**⑮** Click OK.

---

 **TIPS**

### Important!

Use the Loupe to watch small detail and see how the noise reduction affects it. Noise is essentially small detail. Dfine does a good job of controlling noise without hurting small detail, but sometimes it has trouble telling the difference. Reduce the amount of noise reduction when this happens.

### Did You Know?

It can help to take noise reduction off of blacks and very dark parts of the picture. These areas often create a certain structure for sharpness, and a slight bit of noise in them can actually help. As long as these areas remain dark in your processing, noise will probably not be a problem.

### More Options!

Nik Software includes a number of views of how your picture is being affected. In the upper toolbar, you will see something called Views with several icons. The first simply shows you the picture as it is changed. The others may show before and after images, plus split views that show before and after in the same picture.

---

# GET DRAMATIC BLACK-AND-WHITE
## with Silver Efex

Black-and-white photography is a real art. It is not simply a matter of changing a color picture to grayscale or a monochrome. It is about how different brightness values and colors in a photograph are changed to tones of gray.

Nik Software Color Efex has some very good black-and-white effects that offer a lot of control over these tones of gray. But for the photographer who really wants to get the most out of black-and-white, Nik

Software Silver Efex offers even more flexibility and control. The plug-in uses the same type of interface as other Nik Software programs. Silver Efex adds controls to make your work easier in looking at how a color picture changes to black-and-white. Preset effects are shown as small sample images to make your options easier to choose. Just click what you want. In addition, there are a whole range of controls that allow you to make adjustments as needed.

*Note: To begin, click Filter, select Nik Software, and choose Silver Efex Pro. Silver Efex Pro appears.*

● The adjustment that appears in the center pane is the default adjustment, Neutral.

① Examine the sample image thumbnails at the left side to see what looks good with your photo.

② Click the desired change; the center photo shows the adjustment.

③ Revise this adjustment with the sliders at the upper right.

4 Click a color filter to change how colors translate to black and white.

5 Click Details.

6 Change the Hue slider to change how colors are affected.

7 Vary the Strength slider to adjust the effect.

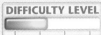

## 86

DIFFICULTY LEVEL

8 Click the Add Control Point button.

9 Click something in the photograph that you want to adjust separately from the rest.

10 Change the Control Point sliders to affect that area.

11 Click OK.

## TIPS

### Did You Know?
Structure in Silver Efex Pro is an adjustment that affects the finer gradations of tonalities. It is similar to Contrast, and definitely affects contrast, but it is a more refined control. Structure looks at and adjusts small midtone changes in tonalities for more or less drama in the details of a picture.

### Did You Know?
Control points allow you to make very specific changes to your photograph without ever having to deal with layers or layer masks. In Silver Efex, you can selectively control the tonality and structure of an object or area. This can really help you define parts of a photograph.

### More Options!
Silver Efex includes a Film Types section that allows you to simulate the looks of 18 black-and-white films. Many photographers still prefer the look of a specific black-and-white film they used when they shot using traditional cameras. This part of the plug-in allows you to try out some of these looks on your photograph.

# Use FocalPoint for
# EASY DEPTH-OF-FIELD EFFECTS

OnOne Software makes photographer-friendly plug-ins for Photoshop Elements. FocalPoint is a plug-in that allows you to do some very interesting effects with sharpness in your picture. A good technique for emphasizing your subject is to shoot with a limited amount of sharpness in the photograph so that only the subject is sharp. This is called *selective focus*.

FocalPoint makes it fun to play with selective focus and other depth-of-field effects. Some of these effects would require an expensive tilt-and-shift lens to duplicate without this program. Plus, performing those effects at the time the picture is taken locks them into the image. With FocalPoint, you can change your depth-of-field effects quickly and easily in Photoshop Elements. Their FocusBug tool literally allows you to click and drag your sharpness effects on the photograph.

① Click File.

② Select Automation Tools.

③ Choose FocalPoint.

FocalPoint opens.

④ Click the FocusBug icon.

⑤ Click and drag the FocusBug to the subject area that you want to be sharp.

## 87

**6** Click one of the four FocusBug legs with solid dots.

These control the size and rotation of the focus area.

**7** Drag the sizing legs until the grid covers the area of your subject that you want to be sharp.

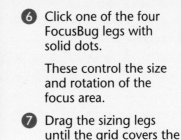
DIFFICULTY LEVEL

**8** Click and drag Amount to change the blur around your subject.

**9** Adjust the Aperture sliders to affect the appearance of your blur.

**10** Click Apply.

**Important!**

You cannot add sharpness to a photograph. If you need something to be sharp in the picture, it must be sharp when you actually take the picture. FocalPoint needs sharpness to work with so that there is something to contrast against the blur. The plug-in can help a photograph with sharpness problems as long as the subject itself is sharp.

**Did You Know?**

You can readjust the legs of the FocusBug as much as you want as you go through the process of refining your blur. Two legs even allow you to adjust the blur amount and opacity while you are working on the image itself with the FocusBug. These are the two legs with open circles on them.

**More Options!**

FocalPoint offers some additional creative options for you. You can create a motion blur to make your subject look like it is moving quickly. You can also add a vignette to make the blurred areas lighter or darker. If the image has no blur, you can simply use the vignette to quickly and easily darken outside parts of the picture.

# Use Enlarge It for
# MAKING BIG PRINTS

High megapixels in a digital camera are not an indication of quality but of how big a picture can be printed. Higher megapixels also means that you can crop an image significantly and still get a good moderate-sized print. Not everyone can afford a high-megapixel digital camera. Also, low-priced point-and-shoot cameras with high megapixels do not have the image quality of lower-megapixel digital SLRs.

Photoshop Elements has the capability of enlarging an image so that you can use a lower-megapixel camera

or crop an image significantly and still get big prints. OnOne Software has a resizing plug-in that is part of its Essentials 2 for Photoshop Elements. Enlarge It uses different algorithms than Photoshop Elements does to help resize images bigger and maintain sharp edges and small details. Small enlargements are fine in Photoshop Elements, but big changes in size are better done with Enlarge It.

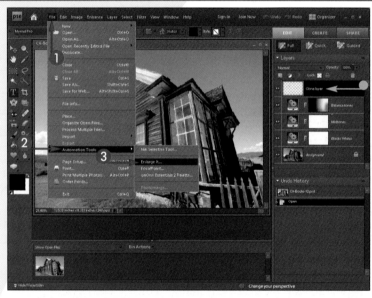

**1** Click File.

**2** Select Automation Tools.

**3** Choose Enlarge It.

● Enlarge It works with layered files.

Enlarge It opens.

● The key enlarging controls are set up similarly to those in Photoshop Elements.

④ Click a height or width.

⑤ Type the desired size for that dimension and click the other dimension.

● The second dimension is automatically calculated as long as Constrain proportions is checked.

● A new image size is seen in Pixel Dimensions.

⑥ Click the scrollbar to move the adjustment panel up and down.

⑦ Sharpen your photo by adjusting Amount first.

⑧ Check your edges for halo effects — bright, unwanted edges — and reduce Radius if needed.

⑨ Click Apply.

**TIPS**

### Did You Know?

Essentials 2 for Photoshop Elements includes two other programs besides Enlarge It. Make It Better uses a side-by-side display of your photo with an adjustment made to one. You simply click the one you like best, and then you get two new photos to pick from. Cut It Out simplifies the process needed to cut a subject out from a background.

### Did You Know?

When you enlarge an image, you typically need to sharpen it. This is why Enlarge It has a built-in sharpening tool. Enlarge It also includes adjustments to affect texture and the appearance of grain in the image, two areas that can be adversely affected by enlarging an image.

### Check It Out!

OnOne Software's Web site is at www.ononesoftware.com. There you will find additional information about all of their plug-ins, including a very interesting program to add special-effect frames to your photos. Essentials 2 for Photoshop Elements simplifies three of OnOne's Photoshop plug-ins to make them a better fit for Elements users.

# Get Photos out of Photoshop Elements

One reason why people photograph is to share their experiences of the world with other people. Photoshop Elements offers a lot of great ways of doing exactly that. Once you have done all of your work on your pictures in Photoshop Elements, you do not want to let them just sit there. You want to get them out so that other people can experience your pictures as well.

Today, you can share pictures with others in so many ways. There are online resources including a new Web site for Photoshop Elements users, Photoshop.com. You can print your pictures so that you can share them with others in the traditional way of looking at a photograph. Displaying your photos on the wall is a great way of sharing your experiences with others.

You can create photo greeting cards based on your own pictures, add photographs to a CD or DVD, and even make picture labels for your CDs and DVDs. Photos on a CD or DVD can even include a slide show of your photographs that you can send to friends and relatives. Photoshop Elements makes it a lot of fun to be a photographer today!

# Top 100

# Gain more options
# WITH PHOTOSHOP.COM

The Internet has become an increasingly important part of a photographer's world. Adobe has created something entirely new for Photoshop Elements 7, a special members-only Web site for users of the program. The Basic Membership is available for everyone who uses Elements, whereas the Plus Membership can be purchased as part of the premium Adobe Photoshop Elements with Photoshop.com or purchased later.

Basic Membership allows you to store up to 2GB of photos online, off of your computer. In addition, you gain access to the invitation-only Online Albums. Online Albums let you upload images that your friends and family can open through a special password. This lets you easily work on images in Elements and then get them to a place where others can see them quickly, too. Finally, Basic Membership allows you to view your uploaded photos from anywhere that you can access the Internet.

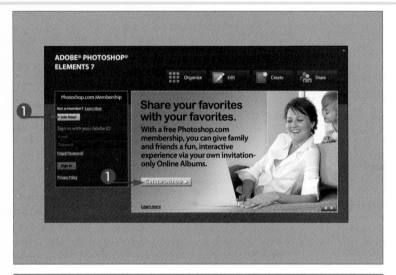

*Note: Start by opening Photoshop Elements. You must have a computer connected to the Internet to continue.*

① On the opening screen, click Join Now or Get Started Now.

*Note: The choices are simply different buttons for the same option.*

The Photoshop.com membership page opens.

② Fill out all the information required.

③ Check the Terms and Agreements statement (■ changes to ☑).

④ Click Create Account.

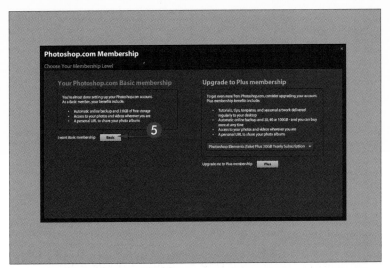

The Membership Level page opens.

**5** Click Basic.

You can click Plus, but there will be an additional charge.

The Account Created page opens, summarizing your account.

**# 89**

**DIFFICULTY LEVEL**

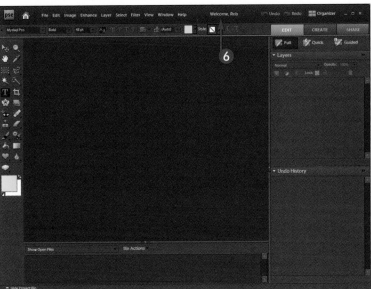

Your account is at the address you chose when you signed up.

**6** Check on your account at any time by clicking the Welcome link at the top of Photoshop Elements.

This will remind you of your Photoshop.com address and summarize details of your account.

---

## TIPS

### Check It Out!

For more information on Photoshop.com for both the Plus and Basic Memberships, you can go to www.adobe.com and click the blue PSE Photoshop Elements icon. Or you can type **www.adobe.com/products/photoshopelwin** directly. There you will see a complete comparison of Basic and Plus.

### Did You Know?

Plus Membership offers you creative templates updated continually, seasonal artwork, tutorials, and interactive Online Album templates. These can be fun ways to work with Photoshop Elements, but not every photographer is going to find them useful.

### Did You Know?

When comparing Plus and Basic storage, you cannot simply use Adobe's numbers. There is no such thing as a standard JPEG file, so all storage numbers must be qualified. The 2GB of Basic is a very low number and can be used only for a limited number of photos. The 20GB of Plus obviously offers you ten times the storage.

**Chapter 10: Get Photos out of Photoshop Elements** 217

# PROTECT YOUR PHOTOS
## with online backup

Backing up your photos is very important. Although neither the 2GB available for the Basic Membership of Photoshop.com nor the 20GB from Plus can replace an accessory hard drive, this online backup can serve a very useful purpose. You can keep special archived images here separate from your home files. Hopefully, you will never experience fire, floods, hurricanes, tornadoes, or any other disaster, but if anything should happen, your images backed up online will give you something to recover.

You can certainly back up any of your photos at any time. This works best if you are only shooting JPEG images. If you shoot RAW, your online backup fills in a hurry. You can get the most from Photoshop.com online backup by creating a special album for backup and then saving finished images there as JPEG files. This is a fine use of JPEG, as an archival format to keep files small for storage.

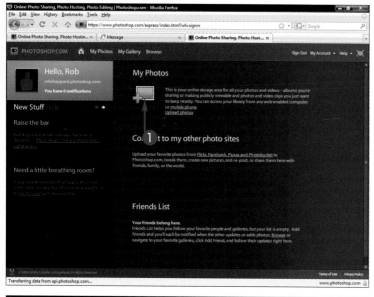

**Note:** *To begin, open your Web browser, go to Photoshop.com, and log in to your account. Your storage site appears.*

① Click the My Photos icon.

The Upload Photos dialog box appears.

② Click Upload Photos.

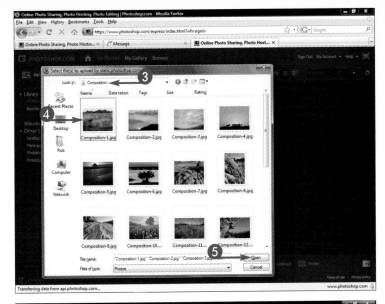

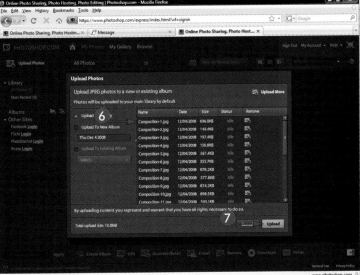

The Select Files window opens.

③ Click the Look In box to navigate to the picture folder you want to back up.

④ Select the photos you want.

⑤ Click Open.

The Upload Photos window appears.

⑥ Check to be sure your photos are correct for uploading.

⑦ Click Upload.

Your photos are uploaded for storage on Photoshop.com.

# TIPS

## Caution!
Never rely only on one form of backup, especially only online. Even if you could get enough storage space online, you would always have to have online access in order to use that storage. Although online access is mostly reliable, it is never as reliably accessible as a hard drive plugged directly into your computer.

## Try This!
JPEG files are excellent for archival backup because they let you reduce the size of your photos. Keep your photo compression low, that is, Quality set to 8 or higher in the JPEG Save options box. These should be files you have finished working on. Avoid reprocessing already-processed JPEG files. If you want to save an unprocessed file, you can use JPEG, too, and then save as a TIFF or PSD file if opened for processing and you need to resave the file.

## More Options!
If you are connected to the Internet, Photoshop Elements will continue to give you messages about things available on Photoshop.com and other offers. To change this, go to the Edit menu and choose Preferences and then Adobe Partner Services. You can check or uncheck a whole series of options for what Adobe will send you under Check for Services.

# ACCESS YOUR PHOTOS
## anywhere Internet service is available

You can access online storage anywhere that you have Internet access. If you travel a lot, this is a great way to get at your photos from a distance. Even if you do not have a laptop with you, you can access your photos using someone else's computer or even the guest computers at a hotel.

In addition, very small, compact laptops, the so-called "web computers," are becoming popular with travelers. Designed for the ubiquitous Internet access

that has become a part of the world today, Web computers have limited storage space built into the units. Because storage is restricted, you cannot take a lot of photos with you on them. Having online storage then makes great use of such computers.

Finally, many business travelers have no need to take their photos with them, but it is nice to access special images, such as of family, friends, and events, while on the road.

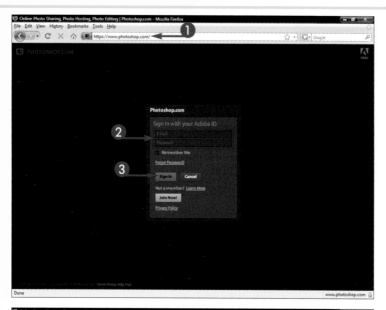

**①** Go to www.photoshop.com.

The login box appears.

**②** Sign in with your e-mail address and password.

**③** Click Sign In.

Your Photoshop.com account appears.

● Your most recent photos show up as thumbnails.

How many show up depends on how many photos you have uploaded.

**④** Click My Photos.

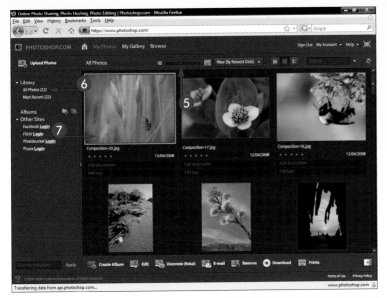

Your photos are now accessible for work.

**5** Click the sizing slider to change the size of the thumbnails.

**6** Click appropriate parts of the Library category to access groups of your photos.

**7** Double-click a photo to work on it remotely.

A simple Edit screen appears on Photoshop.com.

**8** Click adjustment commands to adjust your photo.

**9** Click Return to My Photos to return to your complete library of photos at Photoshop.com.

**TIPS**

### Did You Know?

If you find you are running out of room for your photos, you can always rent additional space. Click My Account and then Account Settings at the upper right of your Photoshop.com page. This opens an account summary. Click the Buy More button at the right of your storage slider.

### Try This!

Photoshop.com is set up for sharing and makes it easy for you to do this. You can create a Friends List. This gives you immediate notification if anyone on this list updates galleries or adds images to their Photoshop.com account. You can set this up after browsing other public galleries and interact with people who have photography you like.

### Did You Know?

My Photos, My Gallery, and Browse are three buttons that give quick access to certain parts of Photoshop.com. My Photos shows you all of your images and lets you work on them, including moving or deleting. My Gallery displays your photos in the gallery theme you choose; this is the gallery others see. Browse lets you browse other photographers' public galleries.

# Create online
# PHOTO ALBUMS

Just like you did in the Organizer, you can create albums or special collections of your photos in the library of your Photoshop.com site. When you upload images directly to Photoshop.com, they enter the library, which only gives you very basic organization. Albums not only let you group and find specific photos faster, but they also allow you to help friends and relatives find them. Albums have no effect on your photos on Photoshop.com other than to group them.

Photos can go in more than one album, too, which gives you great options for organizing them online. You could group photos by type, event, people, and so on.

Albums are a key part of your Photoshop.com image storage. You need albums in order to use many of the sharing features, such as galleries. You can have an album open to all, open only to friends, or private.

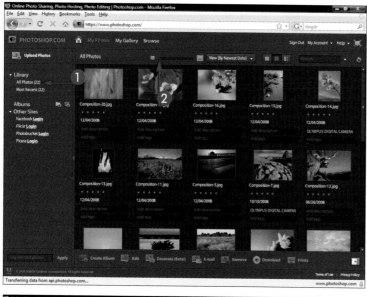

*Note:* To begin, open your Photoshop.com account and click My Photos on the opening page.

① Click All Photos in your library to make them visible.

② Adjust the size slider so the pictures are small and you can see many at once.

③ Press Ctrl while you click several photos to make a selection of them.

④ Click and drag them onto the New Folder icon.

A plus sign appears when you are directly over the folder.

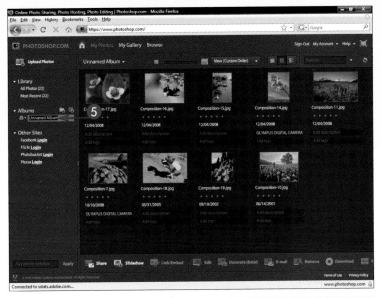

Your new album is created and appears under Albums.

**5** Type a name for your album.

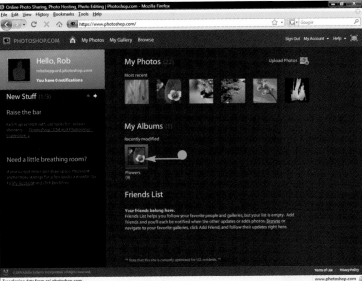

● Your album now shows up on your Photoshop.com home page.

## TIPS

### Did You Know?

You can create an instant slide show of your photos when they are in an album. Once you open an album, you will find a slide show icon at the bottom left of the thumbnail viewing area; click that icon to create a slide show from that album. This creates a fun, 3D, rotating slide show with an option panel on the right.

### Try This!

You can also set up an album without selecting photos. When in the library, click the Create Album icon at the bottom of your screen. This lets you set up and name an album. You can then go through your library and drag photos onto the name of your new album to add photos to the album.

### More Options!

You can upload an album directly when you create an album in Organizer. Be sure that Backup/ Synchronize is checked when the Album Details panel is open and you are setting up a new album. When you click Share, you get a series of options to choose as you prep your album for upload.

# SHARE YOUR PHOTOS
## online

One of the joys of photography is sharing photography with others. On a most basic level, people like to see what others are doing, whether it is grandparents seeing photos of grandkids playing soccer or a business in one geographic location showing how a retail store looks to someone elsewhere. Plus, when big events occur, from weddings to family reunions to births, people love to see the visual record.

Everyone sees the world differently, and photography is a way of expressing those unique visions. Yet, if those photos simply stay on your computer, no one else can benefit from your point of view. Photoshop.com gives you the chance to share photos with not only friends and neighbors, but also people who share your love of photography. You have total control, too, of how people access your photos so you never have to worry about the wrong people seeing specific photos.

*Note:* To begin, open your Photoshop.com account and click My Photos on the opening page.

① Click the small arrow to the left of the album name.

A drop-down menu appears.

② Choose how you want to share your album.

③ Click All Photos to show your library.

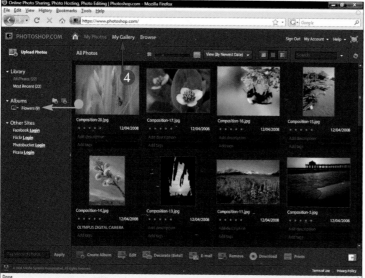

● A new icon appears at the front of your album based on your sharing choice.

④ Click My Gallery.

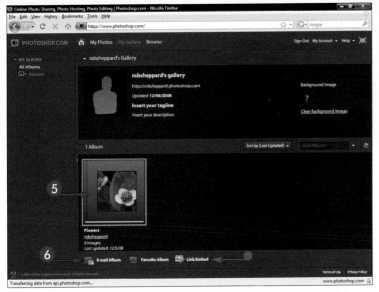

Your My Gallery page appears.

**5** Click an album.

● A series of icons becomes active at the bottom of the screen.

**6** Click E-mail Album to e-mail friends or relatives a link to your album.

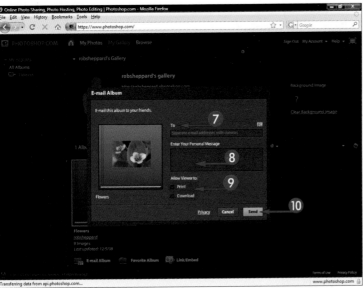

The E-mail Album dialog box appears.

**7** Type the e-mail addresses of the people to whom you want to send a link to your album.

**8** Type a message to let recipients know about your album and so they know this is not spam.

**9** Check if you want recipients to also be able to download or print your photos (■ changes to ☑).

**10** Click Send.

## More Options!

You can personalize your gallery space with a photo of you, plus personal information. When in My Gallery, open your overall gallery section. There you will find a place to add your personal photo, plus include information for public view when an album is permitted for public view, such as a personal tagline and gallery description.

## Caution!

You might be tempted to back up within Photoshop.com by using the Back button on your Internet browser. Do not do it! That takes you off of Photoshop.com and you have to log in again. To move within Photoshop.com, stay within it by only clicking links on your pages. You can navigate to library photos, galleries, albums, and more right there.

## More Options!

Photoshop.com gives you several sharing options for albums. Available to all lets anyone who uses Photoshop.com browse the site and find your album. Private but available to friends allows anyone you permit to view your album, but no public viewing is allowed. Private means that only you can access your album.

# PRINT
## your photos

With all of the emphasis these days on seeing pictures on the Internet, iPods, by e-mail, and other electronic media, one might think that the print is no longer important. That is definitely not the case. Inkjet printers are extremely popular, and paper and ink continue to be sold in large quantities.

And there is something more. The print seems to have a real psychological aura to it. People love looking at prints, holding prints, sharing prints, putting them into frames and up on the wall, and so

on. Prints are important. And photographers are making them bigger and bigger as well.

This book cannot make you a master printer, but the next two pages give you some ideas on how you can make better prints with your own inkjet printer. Photo-quality inkjet printers are available today at very reasonable prices all the way up to expensive pro-level printers.

*Note: Start by sizing and sharpening the photo as discussed in Chapter 7.*

● The width and height are important at a printable image resolution of 200–360 ppi.

① Click File and choose Print.

The Print dialog box opens.

② Click Page Setup.

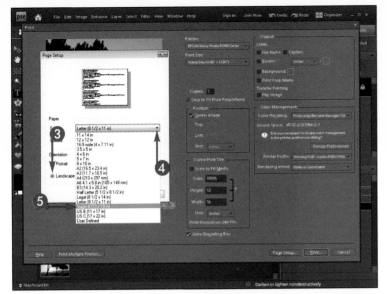

Page Setup appears.

**3** Click Portrait or Landscape for the appropriate orientation of your image ( ○ changes to ◉ ).

**4** Click the Size drop-down menu.

**5** Choose the paper size that you are using.

**6** Click OK.

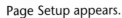

Leave most of the Print dialog box at its defaults.

**7** Click the Color Handling drop-down menu to choose Printer Manages Colors or Photoshop Elements Manages Colors.

Canon and Hewlett Packard as well as lower-priced Epson printers often do well with Printer Manages Colors.

Higher-end Epson printers usually do best with Photoshop Elements Manages Colors.

**8** If you chose Printer Manages Colors in step 7, click Printer Preferences.

---

## TIPS

### Important!

Calibrating your monitor is important. Monitor calibration is done using a special sensor that fits on your monitor screen and reads colors and tones from calibration software. A calibrated monitor gives you a predictable and consistent environment for you to work on images that will become prints.

### Did You Know?

When the printer manages color, it takes the color information from Photoshop Elements and refines it based on the paper used and the color settings of the printer driver. When Photoshop Elements manages color, a very specific interpretation of color is sent to the printer based on paper profiles.

### Did You Know?

Printer profiles are specific translations of color and tonality for printing based on testing of specific papers with specific printers. They are also called *paper profiles*. A special image of colors is printed on paper, and then the colors are read and interpreted by colorimeters in order to define a profile.

# PRINT
## your photos

You often hear photographers say that their goal is to make a print that matches the monitor. Although it is important to have a calibrated monitor that gives predictable results when printing, your goal should be to make a good *print*. No one will care if it matches the monitor or not. A viewer cares only about the print in front of him or her.

This is a different mindset than many digital photographers work with. It means that you have to take your print away from the monitor and really look at it as a print. Do you like the image that you see? Does it have the appropriate brightness and balance of tonalities for the size of the print? Are there color casts that show up too strongly in a print but looked okay on the monitor? What you are looking for is a print that you can be proud to put up on the wall.

⑨ If you chose Photoshop Elements Manages Colors in step 7, click the Printer Profile drop-down menu.

A profile menu appears.

⑩ Select the profile that fits your printer and paper.

⑪ Click Printer Preferences, which is above the Printer Profile drop-down menu.

The printer driver appears.

*Important: This will vary depending on the printer model, but you must set the same things.*

⑫ Click Photo quality ( ○ changes to ◉ ).

⑬ Choose the paper type.

⑭ Confirm the paper size.

⑮ Click the Advanced tab.

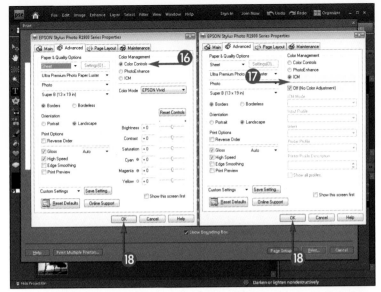

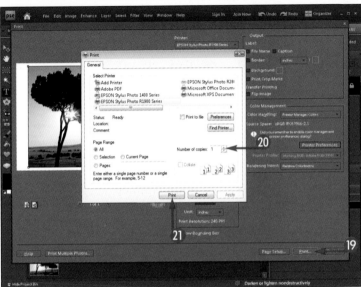

16 If you chose Printer Manages Colors in step 7, leave Color Controls selected in the Color Management section (left).

17 If you chose Photoshop Elements Manages Colors in step 7, select ICM and Off (No Color Adjustment) in the Color Management section (right).

18 Click OK.

19 Click Print in the Print dialog box.

The Windows Print dialog box appears.

20 Choose a number of prints to make.

21 Click Print.

## 94 CONTINUED

## TIPS

### Try This!
Traditional darkroom workers almost always consider their first print a work print. They examine this print carefully to decide what else is needed to make the print better. Many photographers consider a work print a good idea for digital printing as well.

### Did You Know?
Although you can use Scale Print Size to make a picture fit a certain size of paper, use this sparingly. It works if you are making only a small change in size. For optimum quality, you need to size the picture with the specific resizing algorithms used inside Photoshop Elements itself.

### Did You Know?
Printer resolution and image resolution are two different things. Printer resolution is set by the printer driver and affects how ink droplets are put on the paper. Image resolution is set by Photoshop Elements and is based on the pixels in the photograph. There is little direct relationship between the two.

# PRINT A GROUP
## of photos

There are times when you want to print more than one photograph at once. Sometimes you simply want a number of pictures to represent a recent trip. Or you may want to print several photos on a single sheet of printing paper to make your printing more efficient.

This is very easy to do within the Organizer. There you can see all of your pictures from an album or a particular time and then choose the pictures that you want for printing by using the rating stars. It can be hard to select a variety of pictures throughout a large group of images. But you can click the individual pictures that you want to use and then give each one a rating, such as five stars. You then simply sort your images to those five-star pictures. You can quickly process each one for optimum image quality and then select them all for printing.

① Select the photos to print by giving them a star rating.

② Sort to the rated pictures by clicking the star sorting bar.

**Note:** *See task #3 for more about sorting.*

③ Click File.

④ Select Print.

The Print Photos dialog box appears.

All of the choices you made for a single print are also made here.

⑤ Click the Media Type drop-down menu and choose your paper.

⑥ Click the Paper Size drop-down menu and choose your paper size.

⑦ Click Portrait or Landscape to orient your picture and paper (⊙ changes to ⊙).

⑧ Click the Select Print Size and Options drop-down menu and choose the size to print based on your image size.

#95

DIFFICULTY LEVEL

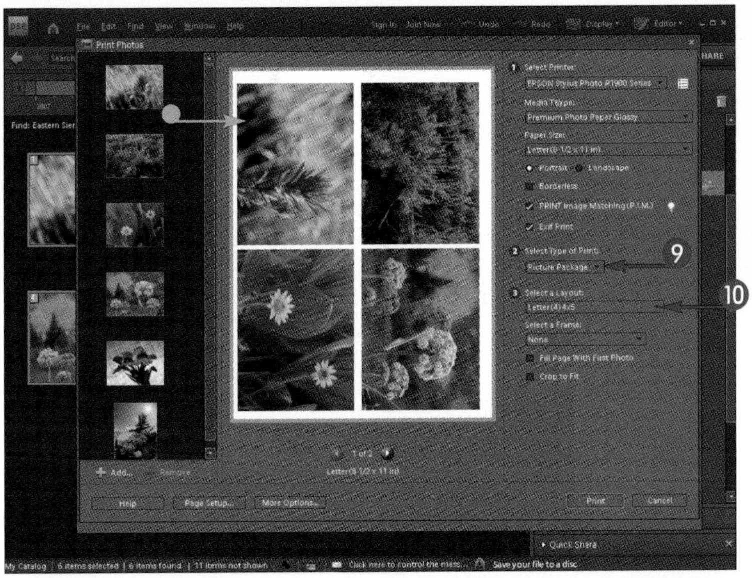


9. To put multiple photos on a page, click the Select Type of Print drop-down menu and choose Picture Package.
10. Click the Select a Layout drop-down menu and choose the layout that you want for your pictures.

- As soon as you select an option from Select a Layout, it appears in the center display.

  To have the printer manage colors, simply click Print now.

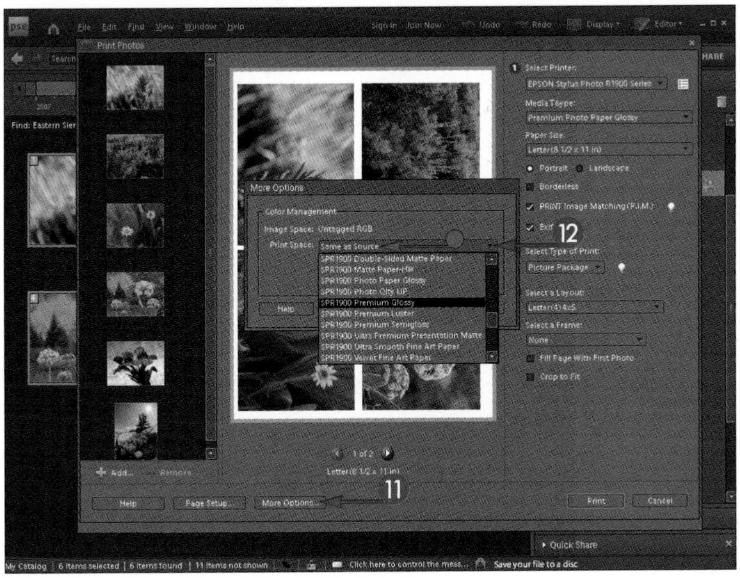


11. Click More Options to print with Photoshop Elements managing colors.

    The More Options dialog box appears.
12. Click the Print Space drop-down menu and choose the paper profile for your paper and printer.

- Same as Source restores the default of having the printer manage colors.

## TIPS

### Keyboard Trick!

Ctrl+P is the standard keyboard command for print. It allows you to print a picture whether you are in Editor or Organizer. In Editor, it takes you directly to the single-picture Print dialog box. A multiple-print button is also there. In Organizer, Ctrl+P takes you directly to the multiple-print Print Photos dialog box.

### Important!

It is very tempting to put in a specific-size print for Select Print Size and Options. If your image has not been sized close to a size that you are choosing, you will not get optimum quality. This is especially true if you are making larger prints. For small, casual prints, having Print Photos size your pictures is fine.

### Did You Know?

PRINT Image Matching and Exif Print are two features that recognize the metadata many cameras record when a picture is taken, metadata that influences how a print is made. It never hurts to leave these checked, and for casual JPEG prints, they can help if your camera has this feature.

# Make a photo
# GREETING CARD

As a digital photographer, you are taking lots of pictures. After all, it costs nothing to take pictures digitally once you own the camera and memory card. But what do you do with all those pictures? One way of using your pictures is to create your own greeting cards based on your photographs.

This really gives a personal touch to a greeting card. You can make greeting cards for events such as birthdays or seasons such as Christmas. You can create cards that have unique photographs for each recipient, or you can create cards with a standard image that you really like a lot. Customizing these cards is also easy by adding text appropriate to the event or something special for the recipient of the card. You can even set up a card and save it so that it can be reused in the future with slight changes.

① Click the Create tab.

② Click the Projects tab.

③ Click More Options.

④ Select Greeting Card.

The Greeting Card panel appears.

⑤ Choose a Page Size for your card.

⑥ Choose a Theme by clicking the thumbnail.

This affects how your image appears and what is around it.

⑦ Choose a Layout by clicking a thumbnail.

This affects the way your picture is arranged on the page.

⑧ Click Done.

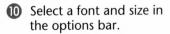

The photo is now displayed as a card based on your theme and layout choices.

**9** Click the Type tool in the toolbox.

**10** Select a font and size in the options bar.

**11** Select a color by clicking the type color and using the Select Color drop-down panel that opens.

**12** Click in the photograph and type your text.

**13** Click the Edit tab to gain more control over your text.

The Full Edit panel appears.

● Your text and photograph are now in layers.

**14** Double-click the T or Type tool in the type layer to select the text.

**15** Position your cursor outside of the text area, and then click and drag to move the text around.

**16** Change any attribute of the text in the options bar.

## TIPS

### Try This!
If you save your greeting card as a PSD file with layers, you can always go back and revise your text. A text layer can be changed at any time. Simply double-click the T or Type tool in the layer and your text will be selected. This allows you to use the standard greeting, for example, and then personalize a name.

### Important!
Process your photo first before you create a greeting card. You want your pictures to look their best when printed out as a greeting card. In order to do that, do your processing in Edit the way you would work on any photograph.

### More Options!
Text works the way it does in a text program like Word. The options bar has all of the standard features of text editing, including the ability to choose a font, size of font, alignment of text, and color. In addition, you can select a style, curve the text, and run the text vertically.

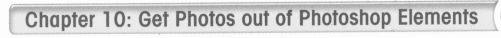
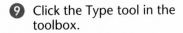

# Create
# PHOTO COLLAGES

Photo collages are a way of putting together multiple pictures on a page. This can be an interesting way of showing off an event, for example, on a single page. Similarly, you can put single shots of all of the players from a kids' soccer team on a single page. This can make a great print that can be shared with the entire team. Photoshop Elements makes this easy to do.

In addition, scrapbooking has become a popular way of working with multiple photographs on a page — which is exactly what a photo collage is. You can even buy photo paper sized to scrapbook proportions for printing.

Photoshop Elements gives you the ability to have some fun with multiple pictures on a page whether you are putting together a scrapbook or just creating a fun collage. This task introduces this topic — you will find lots of things to do with collages once you start working with them.

### CREATE A COLLAGE

1. Open several photos from the Organizer into the Editor.

● The photos show up in the Project Bin.

2. Click Create.

3. Click the Projects tab.

4. Click Photo Collage.

The Photo Collage panel appears.

5. Choose a Page Size for your collage.

6. Choose a Theme by clicking the thumbnail.

7. Choose a Layout by clicking a thumbnail.

8. Click Done.

The photos are now displayed in a collage based on your theme and layout choices.

⑨ Click the Edit tab.

**# 97**

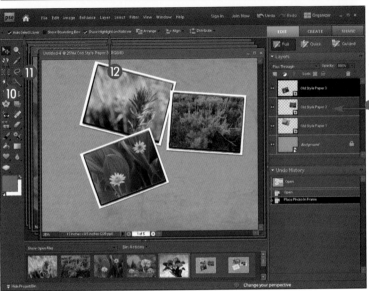

The Full Edit panel appears.

● Your photographs are now in layers.

⑩ Select the Move tool in the toolbox.

⑪ Check Auto Select Layer (■ changes to ☑).

⑫ Check Show Highlight on Rollover (■ changes to ☑).

---

## TIPS

### More Options!

The Move tool has a number of important options. When you check Auto Select Layer, the correct layer is automatically selected when you click an object in that layer. When you check Show Highlight on Rollover, any object within a layer shows up with a blue box around it to help you find the right layer.

### Did You Know?

Photo Collage, like the Greeting Card feature, creates something called a *layer style* to give the edges of the photograph a unique look. Layer styles influence the way an image is displayed, but do not change the actual photograph. This allows you to change an image in a layer and still keep the layer style.

### More Options!

Experiment with the Themes and Layout. When you click these options, you get a small image showing you what the theme or layout looks like, but you really cannot tell how they will work with your pictures until you try them. So try them! See what they look like. If you do not like the effect, close the picture and start over again. This takes little time to do.

---

# Create
# PHOTO COLLAGES

A collage has long been a way of working with photographs. But in the past, you had to cut up pictures and then paste them onto a page. That definitely created problems if you wanted to make any changes!

By working your collage in Photoshop Elements, you can do some quite elegant work. You can move your pictures around, resize them, or add or take away photos, and nothing is hurt or damaged in any way. This is very important because in order to get a good

collage, you need to think a bit about how photos go together. Which photos look good next to each other? Which photos fight with each other and need some separation?

Work your collage with variety to the sizes of images. A big photo or two makes a nice contrast to smaller ones. In addition, resist the impulse to include everything in one page. That can look very cluttered and hard for a viewer to really look at.

⓭ Click and drag a photo to move it to a new position in the collage.

⓮ Click and drag a layer to move it up or down in the layer stack.

This also changes how a photograph overlaps the others.

### ADD A PHOTO BY DUPLICATING A LAYER

⓯ Click a layer.

⓰ Drag it to the New Layer icon at the top left of the Layers palette.

# 97 CONTINUED

● The layer is duplicated.

**17** Click the photo in the Project Bin that you want to add to the collage.

**18** Drag it on top of the duplicate photo you want to replace.

The photo now replaces the duplicated image.

● A sizing bar appears.

**19** Move the sizing slider to change the size of your image within the picture frame.

**20** Click the green check mark.

● You can move the photos around by using the Move tool or by moving the layers up or down in the Layers palette.

---

## TIPS

### More Options!
The Move tool can help you resize your photographs in the collage. Check Show Bounding Box. Now when you click the photograph, a bounding box with little boxes at the corners appears. Click and drag any of those little boxes to enlarge or shrink the photograph. Click outside the bounding box and drag to rotate the picture.

### Did You Know?
It can take a bit of work to get a collage to look right. As photographs overlap each other, sometimes they cover up the wrong parts of the picture. You need to try moving pictures up and down in the layer stack to see how they overlap, better or worse. Then use the Move tool to move the pictures around in the collage until they look their best.

### Did You Know?
Look down in the Project Bin and you see an interesting group of thumbnails that represent the collage. You see the entire process of the collage in miniature. You can double-click any of these thumbnails to see an earlier stage of the collage.

---

**Chapter 10: Get Photos out of Photoshop Elements**  237

# ADD FRAME EFFECTS
## to your pictures

You can apply some very interesting effects to the edges of your picture in Photoshop Elements. You can create very realistic-looking frames, colorful borders and mattes, funky edges, and a whole lot more. All of these effects are applied to your picture as layers, too, which means that they are nondestructive. You cannot hurt your original picture, no matter how unusual an edge effect might be. So experiment freely.

Watch how edges interact with your photograph. You do not want a frame effect more dramatic than your picture. One problem a lot of photographers run into is that they pick a color for a matte, for example, that competes with the colors in the photograph itself. Another problem is that an edge color can be too similar to the colors in your photograph and pull visual energy from the image. Choose edges that complement the photograph.

① Click the Create tab.

② Click the Artwork tab.

③ Select By Type under Content.

④ Select Frames to the right of By Type.

The Frames panel appears.

⑤ Position your cursor over a frame to get a description of it.

⑥ Double-click a frame thumbnail to try it out.

The frame appears around your subject.

● This image has been created as a layer, so blank areas show up as a checkerboard pattern.

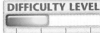

**7** Position your cursor over additional frames and edges to see what they are.

**8** Double-click the frame thumbnail to replace your last frame.

● Alternately, click a frame thumbnail and then click Apply.

**9** Click Edit when you have an effect that you like.

● The Full Edit panel appears with the photo now in a single layer.

**10** Click the background color.

Choose white in the Select Color dialog box.

**11** Click Layer and then choose Flatten Layers.

The background color now fills the checkerboard area as the image is flattened.

---

**TIPS**

### Important!

In order to use frames on your picture, you must have a flattened photograph or at least a pixel layer. Frames give you very odd effects if you work on a standard layered file. Frames are applied to whatever layer is active, but you may not necessarily like the effect.

### More Options!

Because frames are applied to a layer using layer styles, you can repeatedly use a frame with other photos. Save the photo with the layer. Open a new photo. Drag that photo from the Project Bin onto the framed photo. A large plus sign shows you that you are doing this right. The new photo replaces the old one in the frame.

### Check It Out!

If you like interesting frame and edge effects, check out PhotoFrame 4 from OnOne Software (www. ononesoftware.com). This plug-in includes hundreds of frames that were developed by professional photographers but are now available for anyone's use. This plug-in works in Photoshop Elements.

# Make a
# SLIDE SHOW

What do you do with all of the photographs that you have taken? You may print a few, or maybe put some on your iPod or iPhone. Because taking pictures digitally costs nothing, you may take a lot of pictures that never get used. Slide shows let you use more pictures as you share your experiences with others. Photoshop Elements helps you make a slide show that can be used on a computer or projected with one of the latest digital projectors.

Slide shows have a long tradition with photographers. They are perfect for sharing an event, such as a party, or a trip, such as that vacation to the Grand Canyon. A key to a good slide show is to keep it simple. Avoid trying to put every single picture into the slide show. Edit your pictures down to the ones that really matter and then make sure to process them correctly.

SELECT PHOTOS IN THE ORGANIZER

1 Select an album.

2 Select images based on the rating.

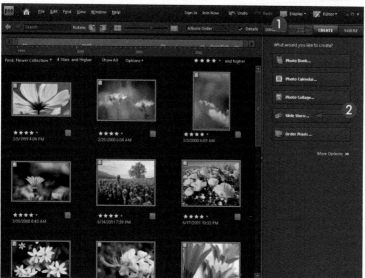

CREATE A SLIDE SHOW

1 Click the Create tab.

2 Click Slide Show.

Slide Show Preferences appears.

**3** Choose a duration for how long each slide appears.

**4** Choose a transition between slides.

**5** Choose a duration for transitions between slides.

**6** Click the Background Color to change the background behind the slide.

**7** Uncheck the captions options unless you have captions in the metadata that must be included.

**8** Leave the Crop to Fit Slide options unchecked.

**9** Click OK.

---

### Try It!

A good way to work with slide shows is to create a special album in the Organizer specifically for a slide show. This helps you keep your images organized and separated from other similar photographs. Rate your pictures, sort them by rating, select them, and put them into the album.

### Did You Know?

Timing in a slide show is affected by the length of time a slide is up, the type of transition, and the length of the transition. A good place to start is a slide duration of 4–6 seconds, which can be typed into the box, and a fade transition of 1 second. You can make these shorter for a livelier show with fast music, or longer for a mellow show with slower music.

### More Options!

Pan and zoom is a way of creating some movement with your pictures. Photoshop Elements zooms into certain parts of your picture, pans along an image, zooms out, and so on to create movement. Give it a try to see if you like it. You can also set this manually for individual slides in the Slide Show Editor.

---

# Make a
# SLIDE SHOW

A slide show should never be simply a group of random photos thrown together. Slide shows look their best with a definite beginning, middle, and end. Even if all of the pictures are of one subject, such as flowers shown here, you still need a picture to use for the first image and the last image, and some sort of logical progression between the images.

You can click and drag any of the images in the Slide Show Editor to new positions. The set of playback

buttons underneath the large window in the Slide Show Editor can be used to preview your slide show without having to output it. This can help you see how transitions are working, if the slides are on too long or too briefly, and if you need to rearrange pictures. Take the time to play back your images as you work on your slide show to make sure that the images go together well.

The Slide Show Editor appears.

⑩ Click the Text icon in Extras.

⑪ Click and drag into position the text box that appears.

⑫ Double-click the text box to get the Edit Text dialog box.

⑬ Type your text.

⑭ Click OK.

⑮ Change the text with the options under Properties.

⑯ Click the audio track.

The Choose your audio files window appears.

⑰ Choose the audio file that you want to use as music for your slide show.

⑱ Click Open.

- The music appears in the audio track.

**⑲** Click Save Project.

**⑳** Name your slide show.

**㉑** Click Save.

This saves your project so it can be reedited in the future.

**㉒** Click Output to use your slide show.

**㉓** Click Save As a File to have the finished slide show saved in its own file.

This slide show is not a project file and cannot be reedited.

**㉔** Choose Movie File to play the slide show as a movie with all slide show features (● changes to ◉).

**㉕** Choose a size for your slide show.

**㉖** Click OK.

---

## TIPS

### More Options!

The Slide Show Editor includes a section in Extras that allows you to add clip art to your slide show. These are mostly little cartoon figures that some photographers will like and some will not. But if you want a fun little slide show about kids, for example, you may find the perfect addition here.

### Try It!

You can create a DVD directly from the Slide Show Editor that plays back your slide show on someone else's computer or in a DVD player. Be aware, however, that DVDs do not always play on everyone's DVD player, especially if the DVD player is older.

### Check It Out!

Although you can use any music you want for a personal slideshow, you cannot simply use any music for public slide shows. A lot of music on the Internet can be used if you are sure that it is copyright free. Or check out SmartSound at www.smartsound.com for music that can be created to specific lengths and used as needed.

# Put your photos
# ON A DVD OR CD

Recording files to a DVD or CD is an excellent way of getting a lot of images from your computer or transporting very large photo files from your computer to some other location. It can take a long time to upload a large group of photos to the Internet, for example, yet those same photos can be put on a disc quickly. This is a big problem if you want to get your photos to a lab for printing big prints. Such photos usually mean very large file sizes.

A DVD can handle over 4GB of data, which is a lot of photos, or a significant number of large image files. A CD is much smaller at approximately 700MB. Either disc is a convenient way to distribute your photo files, either to relatives or to a photo lab for printing.

① Select a group of photos in the Organizer that you want to burn to a disc.

● This can be a use for a special album.

② Click the Share tab.

The Share panel appears.

③ Click the CD/DVD tab.

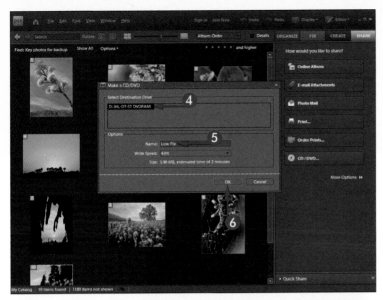

The Make a CD/DVD dialog box appears.

④ Click the disc drive.

You must click your drive even if you have only one.

⑤ Type a short name for your disc.

⑥ Click OK.

A status window appears depending on the disc-burning software in your computer.

A verification dialog box appears when the disc is complete.

⑦ Click Verify.

DIFFICULTY LEVEL

## TIPS

### Important!

If you plan on storing your photos on a disc for any length of time, do not use RW or rewritable discs. Use only R discs. RW discs are made to change — that is what makes them rewritable. You do not want a disc of your photos to change unless you are using the disc only to transfer photos to another computer immediately. RW discs are not recommended at all for long-term storage.

### Did You Know?

Recordable discs can be used for archival storage of images. You are limited as to the number of photos that fit on a disc, so JPEG is a good format for your images. Use archival R discs, such as those from Delkin or Verbatim. Ordinary, cheap office-supply discs are not recommended for archival storage.

### Check It Out!

If DVDs hold so many photos compared to CDs, why would you bother with CDs? Although DVDs work great on most computers, there can still be a compatibility issue where a small percentage of discs will not play properly, especially with older drives. This is almost never true with CDs — they rarely have problems playing on any computer.

# MAKE LABELS
## for CD/DVD discs

If you go to the effort of putting together a nice group of photos on a disc, why not put a good-looking label on that disc? Photoshop Elements makes this easy to do. You can make a label that includes a special photo, text about the disc, and even some unique theme artwork to add interest to your label. Elements includes artwork that can be used for discs that feature baby photos, weddings, graduations, and other events.

You can print such labels out on special adhesive disc-labeling paper available from many paper companies. In addition, Epson makes a number of printers that allow you to print directly onto special printable discs for a very professional look. A great advantage of direct printing on discs is that you do not have anything to align to stick on a disc, nor do you have anything that can come off later.

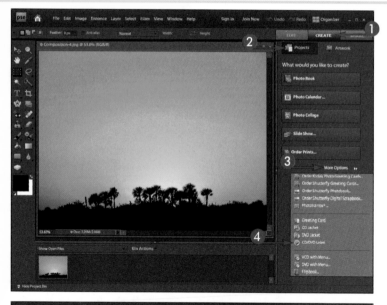

① With a photo open in Editor, click the Create tab.

② Click the Projects tab.

③ Click More Options.

④ Select CD/DVD Label.

The CD/DVD Label panel appears.

⑤ Choose a theme if you want special artwork on the label.

⑥ Choose a layout, which affects how your photo fits the CD.

⑦ Click Done.

A new image appears showing your photo in the layout.

**8** Click and drag the photo to move it within the layout.

**9** Click the Edit tab.

**# 101**

**DIFFICULTY LEVEL**

The Full Edit panel appears with the photo now seen with multiple layers.

**10** Click the Text tool.

**11** Type text over your image.

● This appears as an editable layer.

**12** Change text attributes in the Text tool options bar.

**TIPS**

### Caution!
Never put standard labels on CD or DVD discs. Discs spin at high speeds in a drive. A label must be attached to the disc so that the disc remains balanced. An unbalanced disc can damage your drive. A circular disk print carefully applied is the best way to keep a CD or DVD balanced in the drive.

### Did You Know?
Selecting a photo for a disc label can be challenging. You need a photo that works well as a picture even with a hole in it! Look for photos that have good detail along the edges or at least have nothing important other than space in the center, like the rectangular photo shown in this task. A square photo will perfectly fit the circular format, but it is often hard to find a photo with nothing in the middle that can be cropped to a square.

### More Options!
You can also create interesting printed jacket labels in Photoshop Elements to be used with your CD or DVD box. This option can be found in the same location as the CD/DVD label feature. There is a separate jacket for CD and DVD because these discs typically use different types of boxes, although you could use the same type of box for either.

# Index

# Index

**F**

**G**

# Index

# Index

# Index

# Index

**Read Less–Learn More®**

**Visual®**

# There's a Visual book for every learning level...

## Simplified®

**The place to start if you're new to computers. Full color.**

- Computers
- Creating Web Pages
- Mac OS
- Office
- Windows

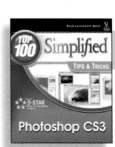

## Teach Yourself VISUALLY™

**Get beginning to intermediate-level training in a variety of topics. Full color.**

- Access
- Bridge
- Chess
- Computers
- Crocheting
- Digital Photography
- Dog training
- Dreamweaver
- Excel
- Flash
- Golf
- Guitar
- Handspinning
- HTML
- Jewelry Making & Beading
- Knitting
- Mac OS
- Office
- Photoshop
- Photoshop Elements
- Piano
- Poker
- PowerPoint
- Quilting
- Scrapbooking
- Sewing
- Windows
- Wireless Networking
- Word

## Top 100 Simplified® Tips & Tricks

**Tips and techniques to take your skills beyond the basics. Full color.**

- Digital Photography
- eBay
- Excel
- Google
- Internet
- Mac OS
- Office
- Photoshop
- Photoshop Elements
- PowerPoint
- Windows

# ...all designed for visual learners—just like you!

## Master VISUALLY®

**Your complete visual reference. Two-color interior.**

- 3ds Max
- Creating Web Pages
- Dreamweaver and Flash
- Excel
- Excel VBA Programming

- iPod and iTunes
- Mac OS
- Office
- Optimizing PC Performance
- Photoshop Elements

- QuickBooks
- Quicken
- Windows
- Windows Mobile
- Windows Server

## Visual Blueprint™

**Where to go for professional-level programming instruction. Two-color interior.**

- Ajax
- ASP.NET 2.0
- Excel Data Analysis
- Excel Pivot Tables
- Excel Programming

- HTML
- JavaScript
- Mambo
- PHP & MySQL
- SEO

- Vista Sidebar
- Visual Basic
- XML

## Visual Encyclopedia™

**Your A to Z reference of tools and techniques. Full color.**

- Dreamweaver
- Excel
- Mac OS

- Photoshop
- Windows

## Visual Quick Tips

**Shortcuts, tricks, and techniques for getting more done in less time. Full color.**

- Crochet
- Digital Photography
- Excel
- iPod & iTunes

- Knitting
- MySpace
- Office
- PowerPoint

- Windows
- Wireless Networking

Visual
An Imprint of ⊕WILEY
Now you know.

**For a complete listing of Visual books, go to wiley.com/go/visual**